Edged Weapons of the Third Reich

1933=1945

Frederick J. Stephens

ALMARK PUBLISHING CO. LTD., LONDON

First published – September 1972

ISBN 0 85524 078 4 (hard cover edition)
ISBN 0 85524 079 2 (paper covered edition)

Author's dedication:

For my

Mother and Father

Printed in Great Britain by
The Byron Press Ltd., 59 Palmerston Road, Wealdstone, Middlesex
for the publishers, Almark Publishing Co. Ltd.,
270 Burlington Road, New Malden, Surrey KT3 4NL, England

Introduction

THE publication of this work marks the termination of seven years of compilation and gathering of information, for it was in May, 1965, that the predecessor to this book *A Guide to Nazi Daggers, Swords and Bayonets* was published. That small work, the first to be published in England on the subject, was simply a basic reference, and which had drawn heavily upon the *1938 Eickhorn Kundendienst* for contemporary information. In the years that followed, it became obvious that this previous publication was in many ways inaccurate, and by no means a true general reference. However, it proved popular with enthusiasts and I received letters from collectors all over the world raising points, asking questions, and correcting some of my statements. The encouragement given by these correspondents led me to delve deeper into the subject, and it is this work that has resulted from it.

The depth of field to study is enormous, and having had chance to research into some areas at length and in great detail, it became obvious that given the time, interest, and dedication, an encyclopaedic work on the edged weapons of the Third Reich could be compiled. The cost of such a study however, would be astronomical to the would-be purchaser and would take a life-time to complete. The course adopted in this work, therefore, has been one of general coverage. Investigating a vast area of study for the more basic facts, I recognise that many of my contemporaries have taken selected topics and explored them in depth. This is a more generalised and comprehensive study which will provide the average collector and enthusiast with almost all the facts he is likely to need. The book I hope will provide useful information for the collector of today and the historian of tomorrow.

Compiling this book involved a considerable amount of cross checking or correcting of that which has previously been published, and presented an enormous task. The assistance offered me by many collectors and institutions lightened the load considerably, and it is with sincere gratitude that I record my thanks to all who have helped. In particular I express my appreciation to the following for their efforts, interest, and above all their friendship.

Andrew S. Walker for photographic contributions, and Chris Farlowe for usage of period publications for reference.

Major John R. Angolia, a friend of long standing, and with whom I have had the pleasure to work with in a great deal of edged weapon research.

The following collectors and authorities have been immensely generous in offering inclusions and helping in compilation:

Norman C. Heilman Jr, Dayton, Ohio; Herman Mauerer, College Point, NY; Ron G. Hickox, Tampa, Florida; Walt Nichols, Tampa, Florida; Marc and Lee Ann Brown, Tampa, Florida; Hugh Page Taylor, Aylesbury, Bucks; F. G. Wells, London; Barry Smith, Bolton, Lancs; Frank Featherstone, Bolton, Lancs; John Burden, Driffield, Yorks; J. A. Morrison, Leicester, Leics; Dr K-G. Klietmann, Berlin; Tony L. Oliver, Egham, Surrey; Colonel C. M. Dodkins, Hove, Sussex; Jack I. Daniels, Gretna, Louisiana; John Scott, Jersey, Channel Isles; S. R. Butler and the staff of Wallis and Wallis, Lewes, Sussex; Les Rawlings and Doug Nie at Weller and Dufty, Birmingham; Tom Greenaway, London; M. J. Godfrey, London; Alan Beadle, Bromley, Kent;

Brian L. Davis, Croydon, Surrey; Phillip Capewell, Brighton, Sussex; Charles Scaglione, Buffalo, New York; Tony Fermor, Bletchley Bucks; John A. Cullerton, London; Steve Bloomer, London; Roger Steele, Hollywood; Trevor Grice, Pontefract, Yorks; D. Dyson, Huddersfield, Yorks; Andrew Mollo, London; Geoff Oldham, Auckland, NZ; J. A. Carter, Loughton, Essex; Allan Bunting, London; Eric W. Campion, Bognor Regis, Sussex; Deutsche Klinges Museum, Solingen; Army Museum, Brussels; Imperial War Museum, London; Library of Congress, Washington; National Archives, Washington, West Point Academy Museum, West Point; Jan Pieter Puype, Amstelveen, Netherlands; Frank van Gelder, Kedichem, Netherlands; Edouard Mester, Brussels; Michael Long, Nottingham; A. F. Harrison, Southend-on-Sea; George Seymour, Southend-on-Sea; Robert McCarthy, New York; Richard Deeter, Los Angeles; E. F. Horster, J. A. Henckels, and Carl Eickhorn, all edged weapons manufacturers of Solingen.

The final word of thanks must go to my wife Joyce, and daughter Nicole, who have put up with a lot in seeing this book reach completion.

Frederick J. Stephens
May, 1972

Note: Only the first and last colour plates in this book fall in sequence in their respective sections; the remainder are placed on individual pages and are cross referenced to their relevant sections and pages therein.

CONTENTS

Army

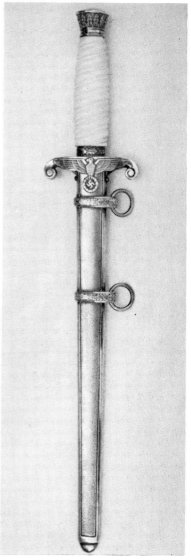

ABOVE: Baldur von Schirach in Army uniform, wearing the Model 1935 Army dagger.

RIGHT: The Army Officer's Dagger. Introduced in 1935 for wear by all officers from Second Lieutenant up to Field-Marshal. The pommel bears a relief design of oak leaves, and the crossguard bears the eagle and swastika motif. Grip is made of white celluloid, though colour variations from pure white to deep orange are commonly encountered. Scabbard is steel, having two brazed suspension bands with swivel rings, and the dagger is suspended from silver aluminium braid straps stitched on to a dark green velvet backing. The buckles of the straps are oval; silver finish with an oak leaf design. General Officer ranks were distinguished by having gold finish buckles on the suspension straps. Commissioned officers wore the dagger with a silver finish aluminium *portepee* knot. Blade is plain, unfullered and pointed. A de luxe standard etched blade, having floral designs was available for extra cost. Overall finish of the dagger is silver plate. Blade length $10\frac{1}{4}$ inches.

5

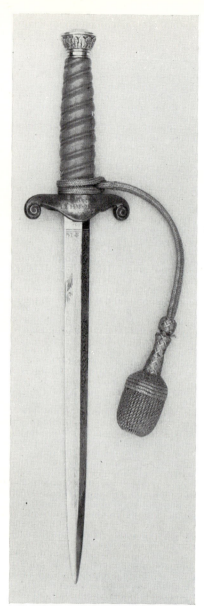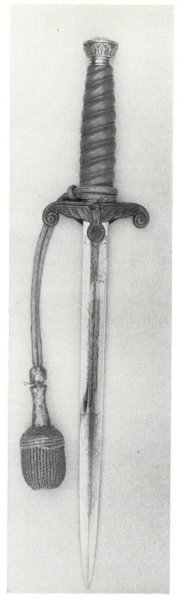

Presentation Army dagger, having the blade etched with an intaglio inscription, and a relief finish floral design. The dedication translates: 'From the Officers and Officials of the Berlin Command, to our Commanding Officer, General Field-Marshal Schaumburg'. The dagger was presented to the Field-Marshal on the occasion of his retirement, January 31, 1937. Manufacturer Alexander Coppel, Solingen.

D. Dyson collection

SA Staff Chief, Viktor Lutze, meeting Army personnel in Paris. Lutze wears the Honour Dagger of the Army, presented to him by his father-in-law Field-Marshal von Braunschitz. The dagger is longer than standard, having a finely stippled hand-finished scabbard. The grip is ivory, with a silver wire wrap, and the pommel is surmounted with the Wehrmacht eagle and swastika. The dagger was presented to Lutze on his birthday, December 28, 1940, and bears a raised gilt inscription on the damascus blade stating that it was presented by the Germany Army to Lutze, the reverse of the blade bears the inscription 'Treue und Treue'. Manufacturer Alcoso.

The straps of the dagger are particularly striking, bearing a silver bullion Wehrmacht eagle on a red shield background, with woven silver oak leaf straps on a dark green background.

Photo Hoffmann collection, U.S. National Archives

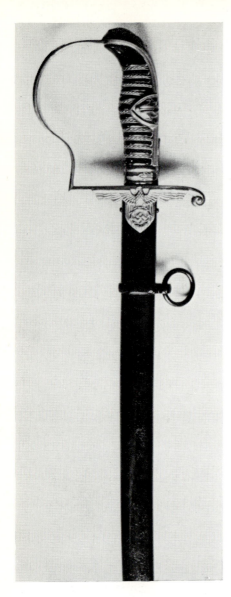

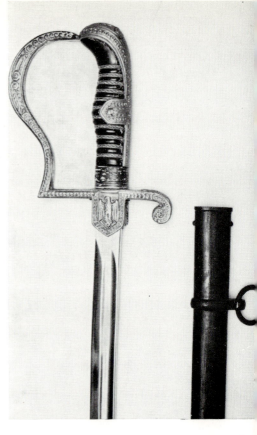

ABOVE: Army Officer's sword, manufactured by the Eickhorn concern, and
sold under the patented name of
'Derflinger'. The hilt is made of cast
aluminium, with a watergilt finish.

LEFT: Army sword pattern 'Prinz Eugen', manufactured by Eickhorn. Although
generally considered to be an Army pattern, this sword was also adopted for
wear by members of the Waffen-SS Division 'Prinz Eugen'.
OPPOSITE PAGE:
TOP: Eickhorn manufactured sword for Army Officers, sold under the trade
name of 'Zeiten'.
LOWER: Army Officer's sword, unidentified manufacturer.

Major John R. Angolia collection

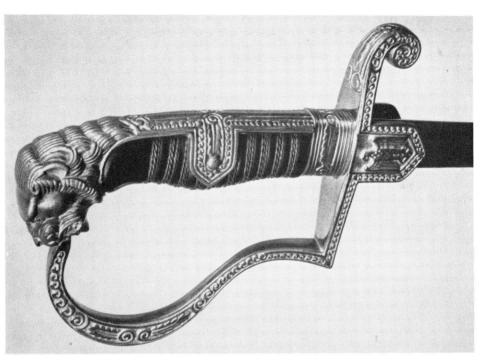

Luftwaffe
(The German Air Force)

RIGHT: Hermann Göring at a delegation meeting in 1935. Göring wears the Model 1935 Luftwaffe dagger.

Photo Göring collection, Library of Congress

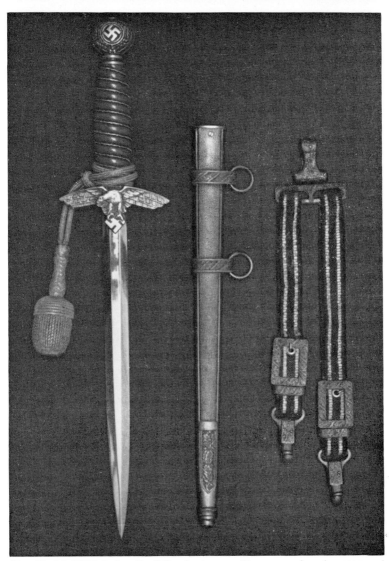

The Model 1937 Luftwaffe Officer's dagger. The pommel and crossguard are aluminium finish, bearing the swastika on the pommel face, and a Luftwaffe flighted eagle and swastika on the crossguard. Some examples of the pommel have the swastika finished in anodised gold. The grip is celluloid over a wood base, and can be finished in a colour variation from pure white to deep orange. Scabbard is steel with a stippled decoration on the body face, with an oak leaf pattern on the face of the drag, the overall finish of the scabbard is anodised grey/blue. The dagger was worn suspended from straps bearing twin silver stripes on a dark grey/blue background, with square buckles. The dagger was worn with a short aluminium cord knot, by all commissioned officers, and after 1940 was authorised for wear by non-commissioned officers without the *portepee*. This example has a deep orange grip. Blade length $10\frac{1}{4}$ inches.

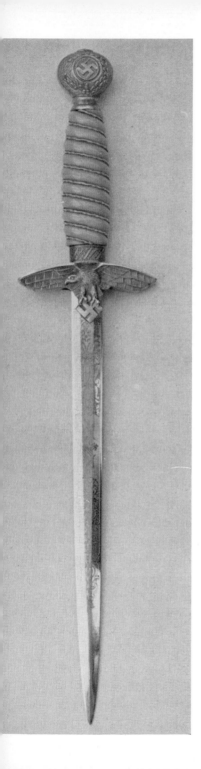

LEFT: 1937 Luftwaffe dagger, having the basic standard etched blade, which shows a Luftwaffe eagle amidst a foliage design.

Eric W. Campion collection

RIGHT: Standard issue 1937 dagger, having a de luxe damascus steel blade, manufactured by Fridericus, Solingen.

D. Dyson collection

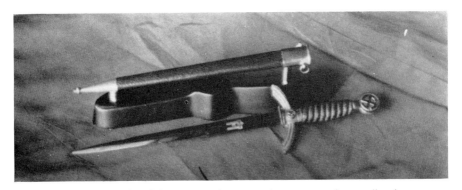

Luftwaffe officer's miniature sword, mounted on a wood propellor base. The sword is identical in every way to the full size version; miniatures such as this and other patterns, were often given away as paper knives to personnel, as a novelty advertising some business concern.

Private collection

These miniatures are shown as a matter of interest and because they are excellent replicas of actual items; they were not, of course, connected with official issue.

BELOW: 1937 pattern Luftwaffe miniature dagger. This example bears on the blade the name of the sponsor of this piece, Besmer-Teppiche, a carpet manufacturing company who gave paper knives of this pattern away, as an enticement to secure orders for the furnishing of Luftwaffe premises.

Chris Farlowe collection

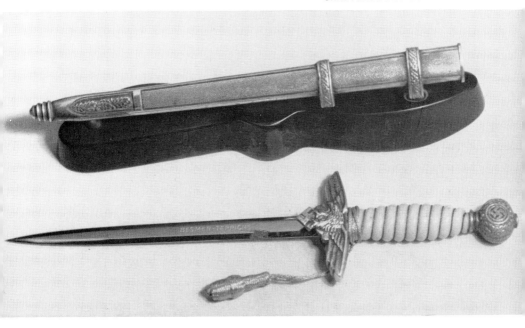

LEFT: Göring in Reichsmarschall dress, wearing the Luftwaffe General Officer's sword.

RIGHT: Luftwaffe Officer's sword, having cast brass pommel and guard, silver plate finish, and blue leather grip. Later examples had die cast aluminium fittings. This example is particularly interesting in that the blade is etched with the inscription: *Oblt. Dr. Heinz Schulz, Vom Offizierkorps der Flak-Scheinwerfer Abtl. 250.*

Major John R. Angolia collection

LEFT: The sword manufactured by the Eickhorn company, and presented by the Luftwaffe to the Commander-in-Chief, Hermann Göring, on the occasion of his wedding, April 10, 1935. The pommel of the sword bears a facsimile of the Pour Le Merite, a decoration which Göring received during World War I.

Eickhorn Kundendienst

RIGHT: Prototype design for a new Luftwaffe Officer's sword, one of a series of proposed new designs which were produced in 1941, one of each example being specially created, though due to the course of the war the new patterns were never adopted or put into production.

Blank Waffen

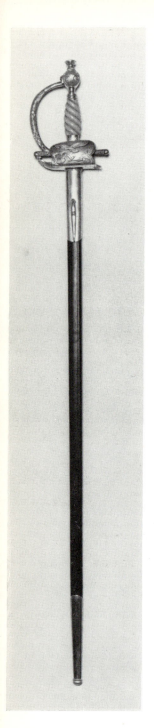

The sword for General Officer ranks of the Luftwaffe model 1938. The first pattern of sword to be introduced was produced in 1935, and was distinguished by having a gilt wire grip, with the Luftwaffe eagle mounted on the grip face. The second model produced in 1938, presented a new design, having a cast brass hilt, gold plated, with a silver Luftwaffe eagle mounted on the folding shell-guard. The grip is celluloid, deep yellow in colour, with gilt wire wrap. Some variations have a solid ivory grip. The blade is finely etched on both sides, with a centre panel deeply blued with gilt finish raised inscription: *In dankbarer Anerkennung* ('In grateful recognition'), and *Der Oberbefelshaber der Luftwaffe Hermann Göring* ['The Commander-in-Chief of the Luftwaffe, Hermann Göring (signature)']. Scabbard is deep blue morocco leather with gilt fittings. LEFT: Sword with and without scabbard.
Chris Farlowe collection

OPPOSITE PAGE:
Blade detail and inscriptions. For a view of this type of sword in wear see picture on page 14.

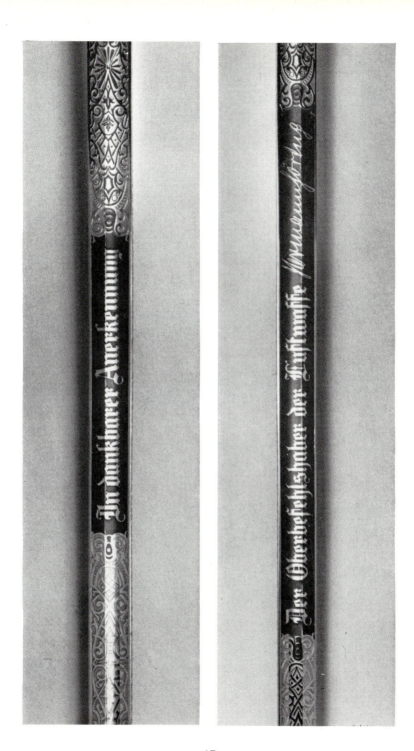

Kriegsmarine
(The War Navy)

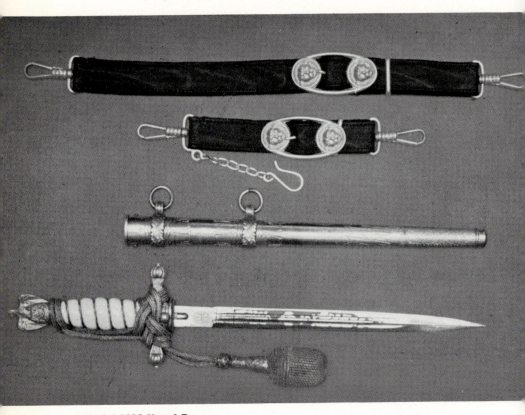

Model 1938 Naval Dagger

The development of the German Naval dirk stems from the official introduction in 1849, of a dirk for officers of the Navy. The original pattern was
abolished during the 1860s, partially reinstated in the form of a midship-
man's dirk in 1871, and then properly re-introduced as a marine officer's
dagger in 1892. It is from the model 1892 that the Third Reich versions
of Naval dagger evolved, with the adoption of new patterns in 1918, 1921,
1928, and finally in 1938. The latter pattern, 1938, was basically a model
1928 dagger (globe pommel) modified by the adoption of the eagle and
swastika pommel.

 In standard form, two patterns of dagger were produced during the Third

Reich, these being distinguished by having either a hammered finish scabbard, or engraved scabbard. The eagle and swastika pommel was introduced on April 20, 1938. Additional to the basic patterns are the 'de luxe' variations, which display ornate blade patterns, scabbard designs, and other varied fitments, produced to the order and expense of individual purchasers.

Basic dagger, model 1938, is shown left. Brass scabbard, hilt fittings, and pommel ornamented with the eagle and swastika. The grip is white celluloid over a wood base, having a gilt wire wrap. Blades could either be plain or etched, with naval motifs and floral designs.

When carried by commissioned ranks, the dagger was normally worn with a white cord knot; the example illustrated has a variation gilt finish knot. Suspension was by means of two separate straps of blue/black satin sewn onto a blue velvet base, and having gold finished buckles. Administrative officials however, wore the same dagger with silver or white metal finish buckles; silver finish daggers are also sometime encountered, but it is thought that these were privately obtained and were not an authorised pattern.

A fine de luxe variation, having a hammered scabbard finish, damascus steel blade and ivory grip, shown with a fine blue/black felt carrying case.

John Burden collection

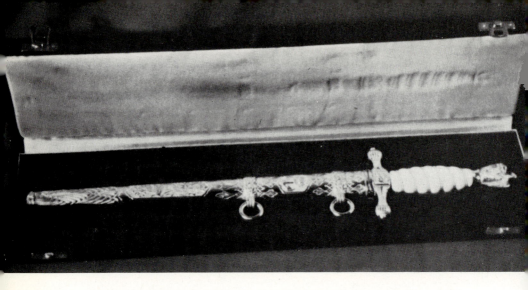

Beautiful example of a presentation Naval dirk in presentation case. The scabbard finish is engraved with Naval motifs and floral designs, and the grip is ivory with gilt wire wrap. Manufactured by the Holler company, the blade bears an etched inscription stating 'In memory of 15th January, 1941, 3rd Company, M.N. Group—North, Ordnance'. The reverse of the blade bears etched designs with a sailing ship motif, an unusual, but not altogether unknown variation occasionally encountered on de luxe dagger patterns. This same dirk is shown in colour on the front cover of this book.

Major John R. Angolia collection

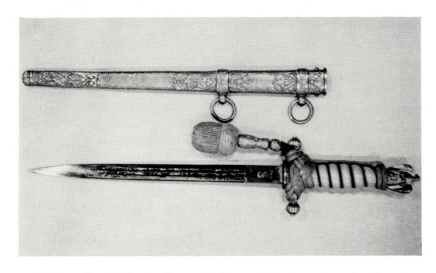

Variation Naval dirk showing a de luxe scabbard ornamented with oak leaves, and standard etched blade.

Weller and Dufty Ltd

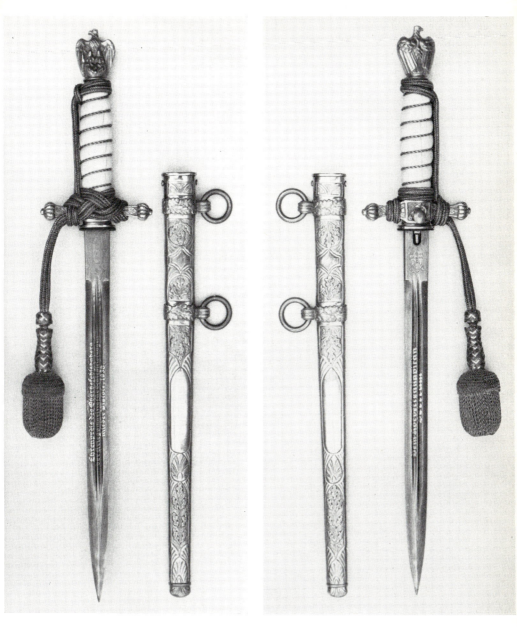

Fine de luxe presentation Navy dagger having ivory grip, and damascus steel blade bearing an inscription indicating that this dagger was an honour prize award for exceptional proficiency in pistol shooting in 1938, and having the Alcoso trade-mark. The scabbard is distinctively ornate, with a profusion of oak leaf motifs.

D. Dyson collection

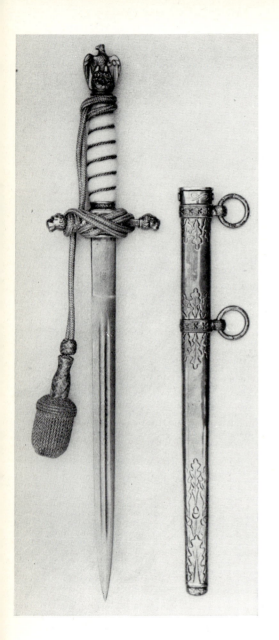
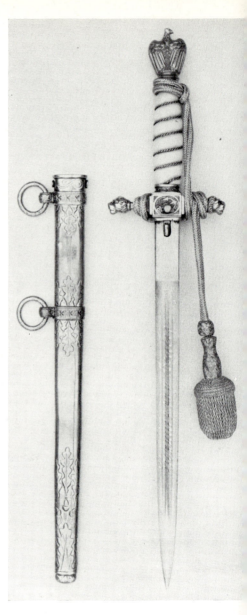

De luxe Navy dagger having engraved variation to the scabbard, damascus blade with etched inscription in facsimile of a signature, and, of particular note, lion head terminations to the quillons. The trade-mark on the blade is that of WKC, and the dagger itself, with the exception of the 1938 style pommel, appears to be quite an early piece.

D. Dyson collection

LEFT: Rare example of the Land Marine dagger, model 1939 having the eagle and swastika on the quillon block.

Trevor Grice collection

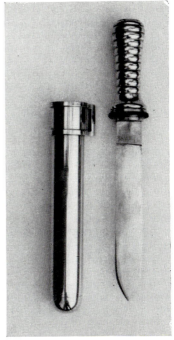

RIGHT: Brass fitted Diver's Knife, a special design which appears to have been adopted for special duty by frogmen and divers of the Kriegsmarine. Marked with Nazi ordnance markings, the diver's knife appears to have been a rare production service item, as few are encountered.

Alan Bunting collection

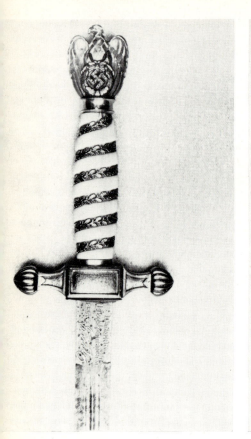
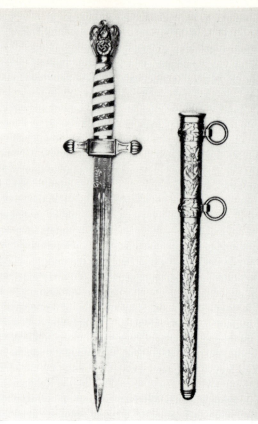

Honour dagger of the Kriegsmarine, introduced by Admiral Raeder in 1938, of which six examples are known to have been presented. The illustrated piece bears the Admiral Doenitz inscription *Dem Tapferen U-Bootskommandaten 9.5.1944,* and is the only known such example. Manufactured by the Eickhorn concern, the blade is damascus steel. The scabbard is ornated with oak leaf design raised from the surface. The ivory grip is wrapped with gold oak leaf band, and the swastika of the pommel insetted with diamonds.

Wallis and Wallis

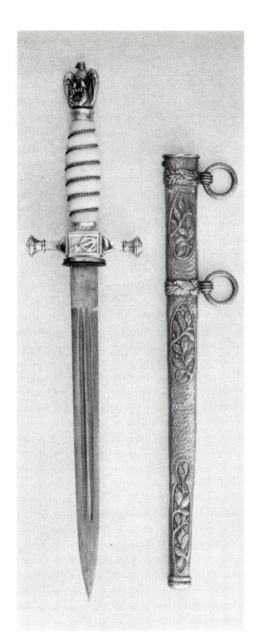

A choice example of a Naval dirk having been modified during its years of service. It appears to have been manufactured originally during World War I (note M1892 crossguard, but made of iron instead of the more usual brass), given the peacetime addition of a damascus blade, with the unusual scabbard pattern bearing seaweed designs during the 1920s, and finally the Nazi-style pommel in 1938.

Eickhorn manufactured Naval Officer's sword, having a lion head pommel, white celluloid grip with gilt wire wrap, and moveable shell guard bearing rope and anchor motif. The scabbard is black leather with brass mounts. Normally manufactured with a plain pipe-back blade, or etched with Naval motifs, this is a rare variation having Wehrmacht eagle and swastika. Designs with a U-Boat motif are also known.

Major John R. Angolia collection

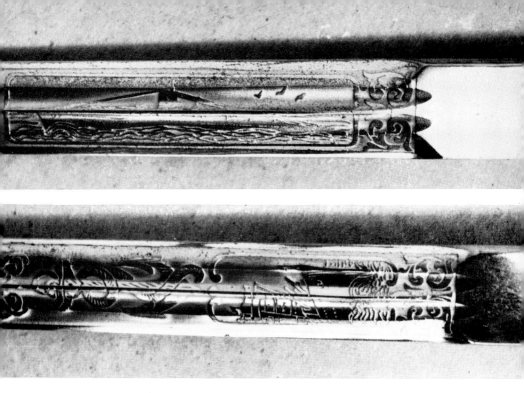

Detail section of dirk blade featuring a rarely seen standard etching, that of a U-Boat. Blade etchings such as this were favoured by U-Boat officers and the U-Boat number was usually included in the etching of the conning tower on the blade. On the obverse of the blade a prow view of a battleship was featured. Although comparatively few of these blade etchings were made, they are rare survivors of the period in that very few U-Boats were captured during the course of the war, and relics from the craft, like the majority of the crews that lost combat engagements, were usually condemned to the depths of the ocean.

John Burden collection

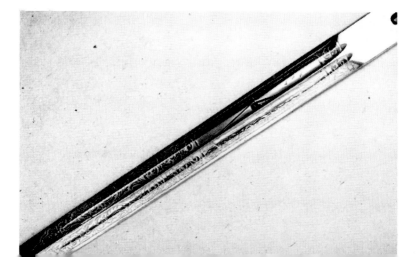

SA
(Sturmabteilung– the Storm Troops)

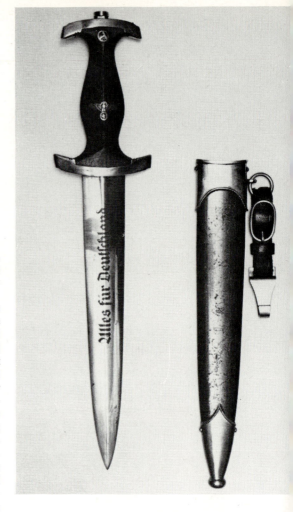

Introduced in December, 1933, the SA service dagger featured a design based upon a 15th century Swiss Holbein dagger.

The grip is contoured brown wood, inset with the SA runic device, and the eagle and swastika emblem. The upper and lower crossguards are bright nickel finish, with a nickeled tang nut sunk through the upper crossguard. The blade is drop-forged cadmium steel, etched on the obverse with the SA motto: *Alles für Deutschland* ('Everything for Germany'). The scabbard is steel, with a brown stove enamel or anodised finish, and nickel-plated fittings. The dagger was worn suspended by a brown leather loop from the single suspension ring on the scabbard upper fitting.

Early variations to the SA dagger were manufactured, featuring such distinctions as no runic inlay in the grip, and unusual face designs of the script for the blade motto. A variation having eagle inlay in the grip with upswept wings was manufactured by the Eickhorn firm in limited quantity during 1934. Blade length: 8¾ inches.

Röhm (left) talking to Hitler in 1934. An enlargement of the picture (above) shows the unusual hanger. The enlargement of a contemporary newspaper picture (below) is the best available of Röhm's unique dagger with both SA and SS runic insets.

During his tenure as SA Chief of Staff, Ernst Röhm was also head of the SS. In accordance with his position, the dagger that Röhm wore featured both the SA and SS runic devices. The dagger was also distinctively ornamented, having an embellishment to the crossguards, scabbard body and fittings, and also an unusual suspension device. Following the liquidation of Röhm in July, 1934, the dagger disappeared and its present location, or indeed if it ever survived the Third Reich, is unknown.

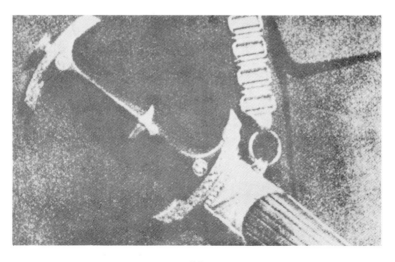

Honour Dagger of the SA, model 1934. Established by decree of the SA Chief of Staff in January, 1934, the SA Honour Dagger was distinguished by the etched motto on the blade reverse, in facsimile of Röhm's handwriting: *In herzlicher freundschaft, Ernst Röhm* ('In heartfelt friendship, Ernst Röhm'). A total of 136,000 SA daggers bearing this inscription are believed to have been manufactured, as well as 9,900 SS daggers. Following Röhm being deposed, in front of a firing squad in Stadelheim prison, orders were issued decreeing that the SA Honour Dagger of Ernst Röhm was now a non-legal accoutrement to the SA uniform, and all inscriptions were to be removed from the blades. Most holders of the dagger complied with this order, either by having the inscription completely polished out, or at least having the offending name of Röhm deleted. A few daggers, however, survived defacement, the example illustrated being complete with the total Röhm inscription.

Frank Featherstone collection

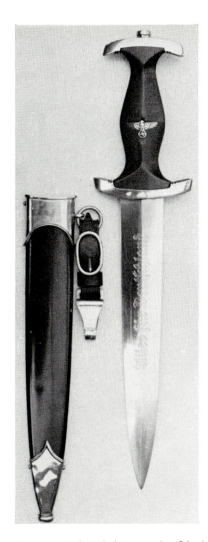 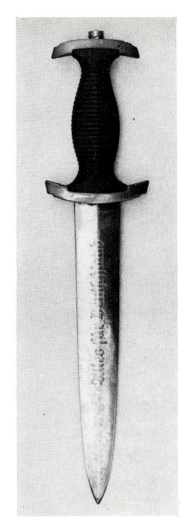

Two unusual variations to the SA dagger. LEFT: Basic early pattern SA dagger, devoid of runic inlay in the grip.   *John Burden collection*

RIGHT: This SA type dagger has the most striking feature of being without either runic or eagle inlay, the grip being horizontally ribbed. Close examination of the grip revealed that no emblems had either been inlaid, or mounted on the surface at any time. The alloy hilt fittings are also unusual, bearing distinct traces of a watergilt finish to the surface, instead of the more usual nickel-plate. No maker's mark.

Two examples of privately dedicated daggers. LEFT: SA dagger bearing etched inscription 'Our beloved comrade Oskar Schmidt, in memory of his Wedding Day, 23.4.36'. Note the reference to Marine Sturm 15/34, the SA marine section. *Major John R. Angolia collection*

RIGHT: Inscription placed on a dagger blade as an epitaph, usually contributed to by the friends of a dead member in memory of their comrade, and which would have been sent to the deceased person's family as a token of respect. The example shown displays 'SA Haupttruppführer Alexander Jurgens, SA Sturm 21/76, fallen on 15.2.1943 at Wilikije Luki'. *Barry Smith collection*

SA Leader's Honour Dagger

Honour Dagger of the SA, Model 1935. The Honour Dagger introduced by order of Viktor Lutze, featured instead of an inscription, as favoured by his predecessor Röhm, ornately cast crossguards, bearing a design of acorns and oak leaves. The right to wear the honour dagger was an award made by Lutze. Acquisition of the actual piece was the expense of the recipient, who was also afforded the opportunity to obtain de luxe fitments to the dagger, which in standard form featured only the ornate crossguards and a leathered scabbard. Extra to the basic cost, if desired by the purchaser, was a damascus blade with raised motto, and ornate fittings to the scabbard.

Major John R. Angolia collection

SA Leader Breuckner at the Berlin Motor Show, 1936 Note the unusual leather strap suspension to his dagger.

OPPOSITE PAGE:
Introduced in 1936, the SA Leader's Honour Dagger basically conformed to the model 1934 pattern, but featured the additional attachment of a chained link suspension. Made of silver, the links featured a swastika design, and the chain terminated in a belt catch bearing the runic SA emblem. To accommodate fitment of the chains a centre scabbard band was utilised,

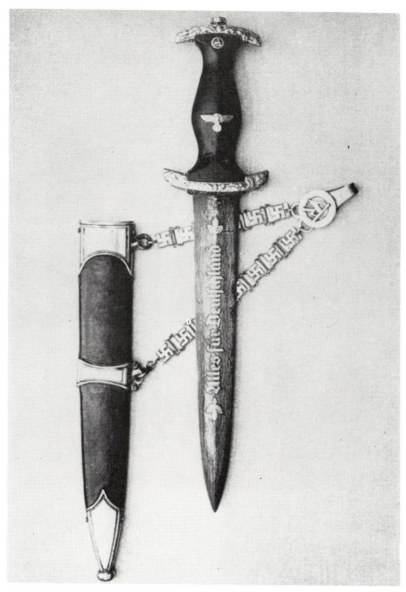

two patterns of which are known; flat extending band on the mount edge, as illustrated; and a mounted fixed ring, as used on the upper chape.

Some variations are known to exist in the link patterns, the SA Staff Chief Viktor Lutze had a dagger that was silver gilt finish, and Hermann Göring wore a variation that has a unique link design, devoid of swastikas and the SA runic emblem on the belt catch.

Tony L. Oliver collection

[SA section continues on page 38]

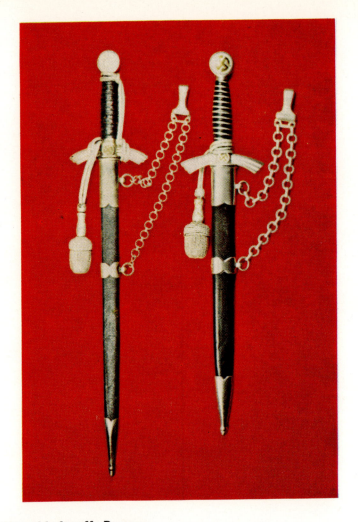

DLV and Luftwaffe Daggers

Model 1935 Luftwaffe Officer's dagger, shown compared to the DLV Officer's dagger (left), which dagger pattern and organisation preceded the Luftwaffe as a para-military air sports organisation. The Luftwaffe Model 1935 was worn by all ranks from Sergeant upwards. The pommel and crossguard are cast brass, with a silver plate or nickel finish. On some examples the curved arm swastika is finished in an anodised gilt. The grip is wood, with a dark blue morocco leather covering and silver wire wrap. Scabbard is steel with blue leather wrap, and silver plate or nickel scabbard fittings. The dagger was worn suspended by ring suspension chains. Commissioned officers wore the dagger with a long aluminium cord *portepee*.

Major John R. Angolia collection

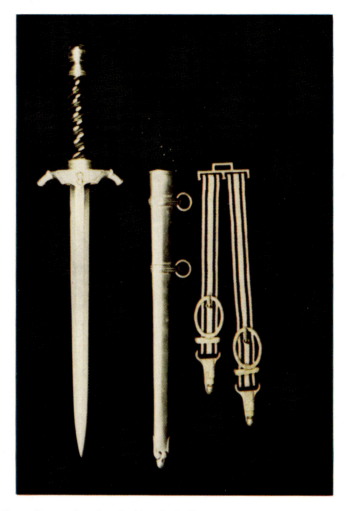

Railway Protection Service Leader's Dagger
Railway Protection Leader's dagger, Model 1938. Like the Model 1935 dagger (see page 88) the piece has the spherical swastika pommel, but presents the distinctive variation of having the winged wheel of the service utilised as the crossguard device. The scabbard is polished steel, and finish could be either silver plate or satin polished aluminium. The dagger was worn suspended by twin silver braid straps, with twin purple/black stripes sewn on to a deep purple velvet backing. A silver knot with purple weave was also worn. See also page 89.

Major John R. Angolia collection

[continued from page 35]

Herman Göring, in SA uniform, and wearing his own particular variation of the SA dagger. Göring wore this dagger on Reich Party Day in 1936 (illustrated), 1937, and 1938. This was possibly the last occasion on which the Commander-in-Chief of the German Air Force appeared in SA Party uniform, as the Reich Party Day Rally for 1939 was cancelled about ten days before it was due to take place, owing to the imminent possibility of the outbreak of war.

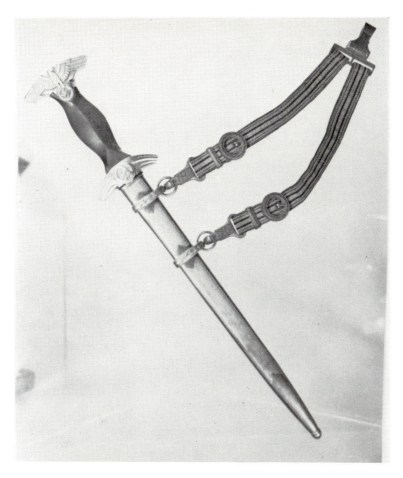

The dagger of the SA Standarte Feldherrnhalle, introduced in 1937. This newly distinctive pattern, described at the time as the 'new dagger for SA Leaders', was worn only by members of the elite Feldherrnhalle, bearing the rank of Major and above. Manufactured by the Eickhorn concern, the total quantity of these daggers is believed not to have exceeded 50. The metal fittings of the hilt are die-cast aluminium, custom fitted to the brown bakelite grip. The eagle and swastika design on the pommel section is repeated on both sides, the crossguard bears the SA runic emblem only on the obverse. The blade bears the etched motto *Alles für Deutschland*. The scabbard is pressed steel, with an oak leaf design on the suspension ring mounts. The whole of the metal portion of the dagger is watergilt finish. The dagger is worn suspended from twin gold braid straps with brown stripes, and bears oak leaf circular buckles.

W. Roy Evans collection

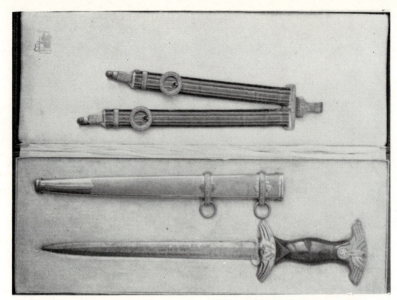

The Feldherrnhalle Dagger presented to SA Staff Chief Viktor Lutze shown in its presentation case. This unique piece has a brown wood grip, with hand cut steel pommel and crossguard gold plated. Although Lutze was the chief of all the SA, he was not the chief of the Feldherrnhalle; it was Göring to whom this capacity was given. The dagger awarded to Lutze has a damascus steel blade bearing the dedication 'To the Staff Chief of all the SA, 28.12.1937, from the Fuhrerkorps of the Standarte Feldherrnhalle'. The reverse of the blade bears the 'Everything for Germany' motto. Göring, in his position of Feldherrnhalle Chief, wore his own special version, having an ivory grip and a similar white grip version was also presented to the Italian General Russo on the occasion of his visit to Berlin.

Courtesy Eric W. Campion collection

Reichs Labour Service (Reichsarbeitdienst—RAD) Leader's Dagger

RAD Leader's dagger, introduced in 1937 for all ranks from Feldmeister and over. The hilt is cast aluminium, formed in an eagle's head pommel, and bearing the RAD device on the crossguard. The slim blade is falchion in shape, etched on the obverse with the RAD motto. Celluloid grips are fitted to the hilt, colours ranging from white to deep orange, secured by a retaining screw situated in the reverse face.

The scabbard is made of steel, with silver finish, and a deep blue anodising finish to the stippled area in the centre panel. It was worn suspended from brown leather straps with square buckles. See also page 71.

Major John R. Angolia collection

SS
(Schutzstaffel—The Elite Guard)

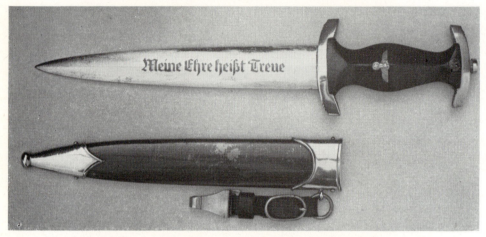

The SS dagger model 1933, worn by all ranks from SS-Mann up to Reichsführer-SS. The hilt fittings of the dagger can be either silver, or nickel-plate, and the black wood grip bears the emblem of the SS, and the national eagle and swastika. The blade is etched with the motto *Meine Ehre Heisst Treue* ('My Honour Commands Loyalty') on the obverse, and usually the manufacturer's trade-mark and RZM control number on the reverse. Specimens without either trade-mark or RZM markings do, however, exist. The scabbard is steel, with bright silver or nickel-plate fittings, and a black enamel or gun metal blue finish to the body. Suspension of the M1933 was by means of a short black leather loop.

BELOW: Detail section of an SS dagger blade, showing variation in which an exclamation mark (!) is incorporated in the motto. This variation appears only to be encountered on blades manufactured by Jacobs and Company, Solingen.

RIGHT: Heinrich Himmler, as Chief of the SS, prior to his elevation to that of Reichsführer-SS in 1934, wearing the M1933 dagger.

SWF photo

LEFT: An example of a privately manufactured SS paper knife. Items such as this were often manufactured to private order, intended to be used as desk ornaments and letter openers. They have no official status in the ranks of Third Reich blades, and are to be regarded more as an interesting curio of the period. The example illustrated is made of steel, with a brass inlay to the hilt, displaying on the obverse face the SS runes and an oak leaf panel, and on the obverse the Death's-head emblem.

Weller & Dufty Ltd

[SS section continues on page 46]

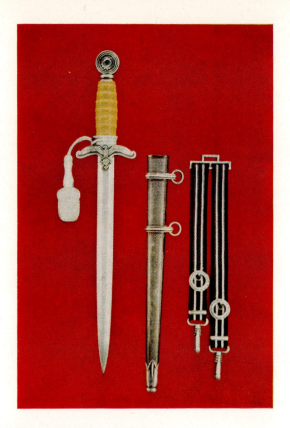

TeNo SENIOR OFFICER'S DAGGER

TeNo senior officer's dagger, worn by all ranks from Kameradschaftsführer to Chef der TN.

The pommel bears the TeNo cogwheel emblem, and the TeNo eagle and swastika on the crossguard. All metal portions of the hilt and scabbard are in silver plate, with a dark anodised finish to the recess areas of the decoration. The grip is made of celluloid, most usually finished in yellow/orange, although pale yellow and white are sometimes encountered. A short aluminium knot was worn on the dagger at all times.

Suspension of the dagger was by means of two basic patterns of strap. For walking out grey braid straps with twin silver stripes, and for field duty plain black leather straps were utilised. The buckles of the straps are ornated with the TeNo cogwheel emblem. For more details see page 73.

Major John R. Angolia collection

OPPOSITE PAGE, LOWER:

NPEA Leader's Dagger

NPEA leader's dagger, Model 1936. A first model leader's dagger having the swivel ring scabbard mounts.

Major John R. Angolia collection

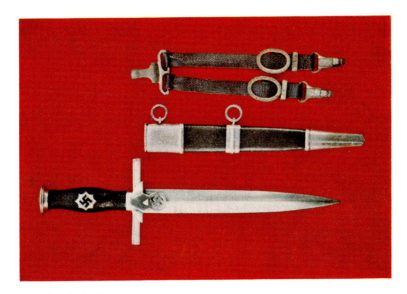

RLB Leader's Dagger

The 1936 RLB leader's dagger bore the same features as the NCO pattern, but was distinguished in that it had a longer blade, with a domed pommel, and blue leather wrap to the scabbard. In 1938, the new pattern introduced carried the new design emblem, on a blue leather grip. The dagger was worn suspended by twin leather straps, featuring the newly introduced centre scabbard band. The straps were twin blue/black leather straps. The example illustrated has the rather unusual feature of gilt finish buckles on the straps.

Major John R. Angolia collection

See also page 75.

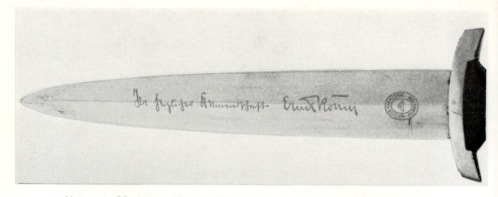

Very rare SS dagger Model 1933, having on the reverse of the blade the complete Röhm inscription. Like the SA Röhm pieces, previously described, a limited number (believed 9,900) of SS personnel became authorised to wear the SA/SS Honour Dagger. As detailed in the orders following Röhm's execution, all holders of the Röhm Honcur Dagger were instructed to have the inscription removed, most of whom complied with the order. A very few had only the offending portion of Röhm's name removed, though this was unusual for SS members who were generally opposed to Röhm and had little support for his ambitions in making the SA the leading political army of the Reich. The illustrated piece is the only example of the SS model 1933 with a complete unmutilated Röhm inscription that the author has ever seen, though quite possibly other examples may exist.

Private collection

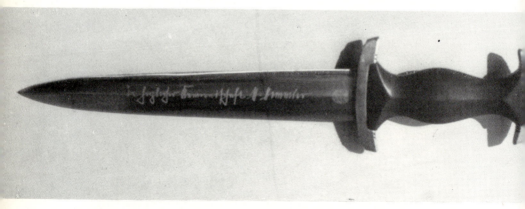

SS dagger bearing the Himmler honour inscription. The award of these pieces came about in 1934, following the liquidation of Röhm. Himmler, who by now had been raised to the position of Reichs Leader of SS, authorised the award of these daggers, which bore on the reverse of the blade a facsimile of Himmler's handwriting, bearing the dedication *In Herzlicher Kameraden-schaft H. Himmler* ('In heartfelt comradeship, H. Himmler').

F. G. Wells collection

An example of the very rare early pattern SS Honour Sword. Manufactured by the Eickhorn company, this piece was probably produced in 1935. The hilt is made of white metal, ornated with a lioness head pommel, and bearing on the obverse crossguard the eagle and swastika, and on the reverse the SS runes, inlaid in black and white enamel. The blade bears the SS motto etched in relief, and contained within a panel surround. The wearing of this pattern sword was abolished in 1938, when the newly introduced Degen pattern was adopted by the SS, and in which series an etched blade honour sword was produced.

SS Service dagger Model 1936. It is distinguished from the Model 1933 by the fine ornate silver-plated links which bear the siegrune SS and a death's head device. The links attach to a belt loop in the style of a four-loop knot. The Model 1936 was authorised for wear by all SS officers, and all SS men who had been members of the SS for three years or more. The knot, as shown attached, was worn only by Waffen-SS personnel serving with Army Units, and was authorised as an attachment to the dagger in 1941.

LEFT: Herman Fegelein and the leader of the SS Leibstandarte Adolf Hitler, Josef Dietrich. Fegelein wears the Model 1933 dagger, whilst Dietrich wears the dress bayonet, a most unusual dress accoutrement for an SS Leader of his position.

Photo from Fegelein photo album,
Major John R. Angolia collection

RIGHT: Göring in conversation with SS officers. The officer on the right is wearing the Model 1936 SS dagger, distinguished by its chain link suspension. Note that the example shown in wear here is missing the bottom mount of the scabbard.

Göring collection Library of Congress

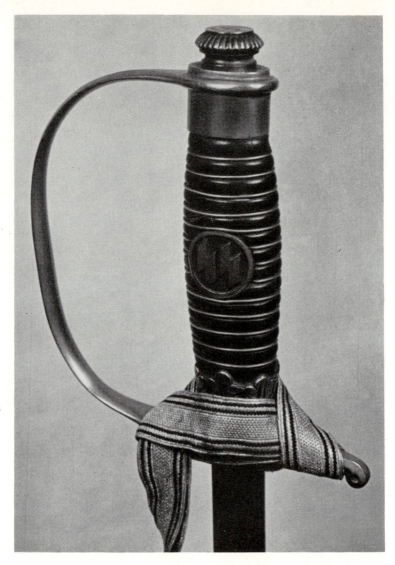

SS Leader's sword. Introduced in 1938 for wear by all officer ranks of the SS, SS-VT, and Waffen-SS, the wood grip is insetted with a silver SS runic badge. This was known as the Führerdegen, shown also on page 51.

Major John R. Angolia collection

LEFT: An officer of the RFSS (Staff of the Reichsführer SS) showing his son his SS Führerdegen. For a detail view of this sword, see page 50.

SWF photo

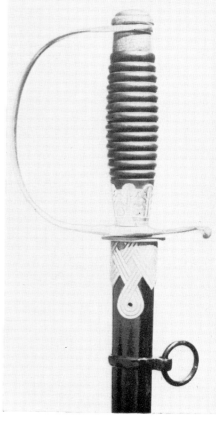

RIGHT: SS Bewerberdegen (Officer Candidate sword). Identical in style to the SS Unterführerdegen, with the distinguishing feature of being devoid of grip insignia. The Leader pattern of the Officer Candidate sword is the same, but has the additional feature of a raised pommel, bearing the SS runes.

NSKK
(National Sozialistiches Kraftahr-Korps— National Socialist Motor Corps)

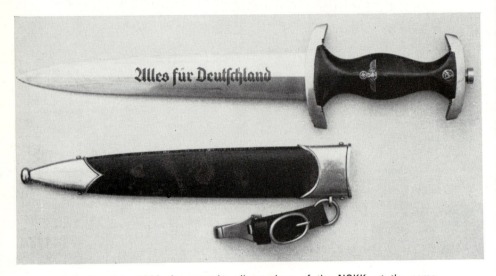

Introduced in 1933, for wear by all members of the NSKK, at the same time as the SA and SS Service Daggers were introduced. The dagger was identical in form to the SA pattern. In May, 1936, an order was passed instructing NSKK personnel that henceforth the scabbard of the NSKK dagger was to be painted black. This became the only distinguishing feature between these and the SA versions.

OPPOSITE PAGE, LEFT:
NSKK Senior Leader's Service Dagger, introduced in 1936. Like the model 1933-36 dagger, the basic knife was identical to the SA version. It did, however, have the extra fitment of a centre scabbard band and a chain link suspension. The face of the links is decorated with a design of swastikas, NSKK eagle device, and in the centre of the lower row of links, a road traffic sign. Two versions of the dagger exist, one having four links on the upper row, as illustrated, and one having only three links on the upper row. Personnel serving in the NSKK Marine Division, wore the same basic Senior Leader's dagger, distinguished in having copper-gilt plating on the fittings.

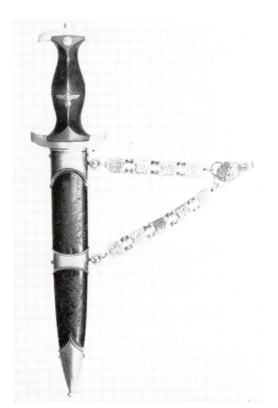
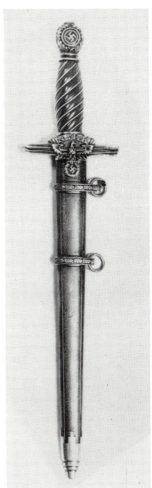

A very rare NSKK Leader's Dagger, introduced in 1938. No precise details governing the production of this dagger are available, though photographic evidence from the period indicates that at least three variations existed. The piece illustrated was manufactured by the Eickhorn company. The hilt fittings are of die-cast aluminium, with a pommel design reminiscent of the 1937 Luftwaffe pattern, though more elongated in overall shape. The crossguard bears the NSKK eagle device. The grip of the dagger is a deep orange celluloid, with silver wire wrap. Blade is plain, bearing only the manufacturer's trade-mark.

Robert McCarthy collection

Hitler Jugend
(Hitler Youth)

Hitler Youth Knife (description on opposite page).

OPPOSITE PAGE:

Early pattern Nazi Hitler Youth knife, believed to have been manufactured by Horster. Longer and heavier than the basic Fahrtenmesser, a number of variation patterns are known to exist. There is no evidence to prove that such pieces are 'Honour' daggers, etc, and all indications are that these were manufactured prior to the adoption of the officially recognised HJ knife pattern. The illustrated item has a steel hilt, bearing an etched panel displaying an HJ Gefolgschaft banner. The grip is black checkered wood. The obverse of the blade features an etched panel with the motto Blut und Ehre! (Blood and Honour!). LEFT: Hilt detail in close-up.

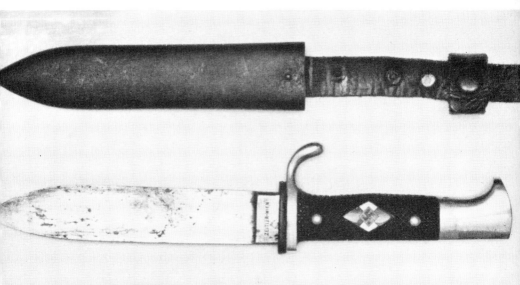

ABOVE: HJ Fahrtenmesser (hike knife), introduced 1933 and worn by all ranks of the HJ up until 1937, when the leader's pattern was introduced, and worn by those whose rank merited it. The HJ knife has a steel hilt, with bright nickel plating. The grips are black checkered plastic, insetted with the HJ diamond swastika. The blade is short and single edged. Prior to 1938 all HJ knife blades were etched with the motto *Blut und Ehre!* Following the introduction of the leader's dagger, the Fahrtenmesser was manufactured only with the plain blade. Blade length $5\frac{1}{2}$ inches. Scabbard is a steel pressing with black leather belt loop.

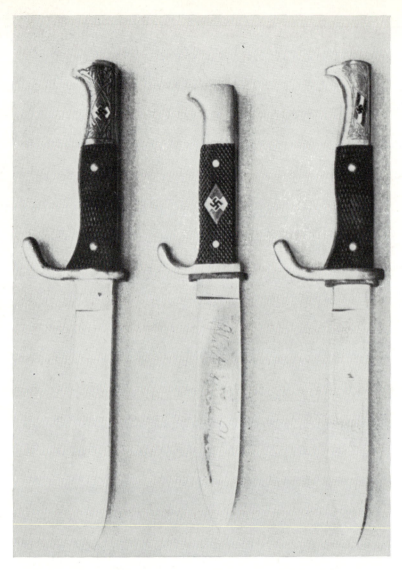

HJ Fahrtenmesser, with etched blade version. shown compared to two early
type HJ knives The example on the left has the HJ diamond inset in the
pommel, whereas the right-hand version has an enamelled inlay representa-
tion of the HJ Gefolgschaft flag.

Tony L. Oliver collection

OPPOSITE, LOWER:
Baldur von Schirach, wearing the basic HJ Fahrtenmesser.

Photo Major John R. Angolia collection

Delegation of Hitler Youth visiting Tokyo, 1938. During the period of this historic visit, members of the HJ wore an interesting variation to the standard leader's dagger. This had a silver finished scabbard, suspended by white leather straps (left). The Fahrtenmesser (right) was worn unaltered, with the exception of white leather strapping on the scabbard belt loop, worn from a white leather belt.

SWF photos

ABOVE: Another view of Hitler Youth Leaders in Tokyo wearing the silver finished scabbard with their leaders' daggers. The standard scabbard is shown below and described opposite.

Hitler Youth Leader's Dagger

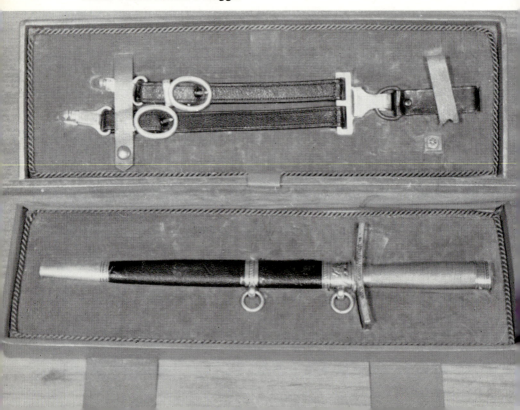

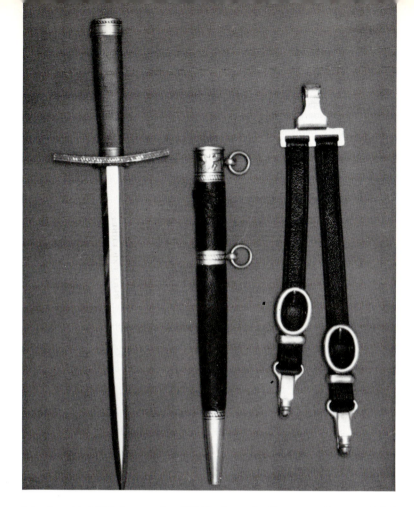

Introduced in 1937, for wear by all HJ leader ranks. The pommel is ornamented with the HJ diamond swastika. The grip is wrapped with silver wire. The blade is straight, and etched on the obverse with *Blut und Ehre!*. The scabbard is steel, with a dark blue leather wrap, and the fittings are silver plated. The upper locket of the scabbard is ornated in relief with the HJ eagle clutching a sword and a hammer. The dagger was worn suspended from twin blue/black leather straps with silver buckles.

OPPOSITE PAGE:

Hitler Youth leader's dagger shown in its original presentation case. The grip is bound with silver wire, and the silver finish pommel bears the HJ diamond. The scabbard is blue/black leather, with silver fittings, the locket of the scabbard bearing the HJ eagle. Blade is etched with the HJ motto.

The presentation case is quite an interesting accoutrement to the dagger *per se*, being made of red leatherette, with the white HJ eagle embossed on the surface of the lid. The interior is lined with red velvet, and custom recessed to accommodate the dagger in the lower section, and the straps in the upper. A dividing flap separates the two sections. Blade length is $9\frac{1}{4}$ inches.

A strange variation, of crude manufacture, of the Hitler Youth leader's dagger. The impression with this dagger is that it is entirely hand made, having a silvered finish pommel and crossguard, with silver wire wrap to the grip. The $9\frac{1}{2}$ inch blade is well executed, though devoid of motto or manufacturer's markings. The embellishment to the crossguard is a zig-zag design, with the HJ diamond swastika engraved on the upper surface. The scabbard is constructed of steel with a leather wrap, and the fittings are made of low-grade German silver, ornated in relief on the locket with a crude HJ eagle.

No details of origin or documentation have been located concerning this piece; its crude (but not amateur) construction give indication that it may well be an original prototype pattern from which the basic HJ leader's dagger evolved.

Private collection

OPPOSITE PAGE, LOWER:
Small type HJ dagger, with HJ diamond on the scabbard, possibly a variation manufactured during the war. Plain unetched blade, length $4\frac{3}{4}$ inches.

Tony L. Oliver collection

RIGHT: Special bayonet worn by Hitler Youth, distinguished by the HJ diamond inlaid in the grip. The blade size is the same as the standard carbine dress bayonet, except the distinguishing feature of the swedge (or false edge) is omitted from the HJ pattern. Believed to have been worn only by members of the Wachgefolgschaft – 'Watch Followers' of the HJ, a wartime unit.

J. Cullerton collection

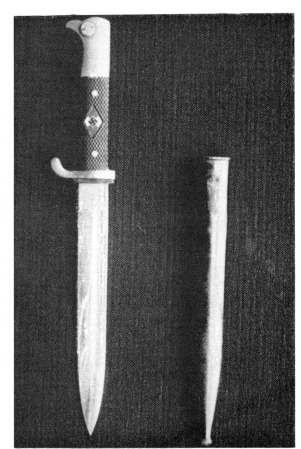

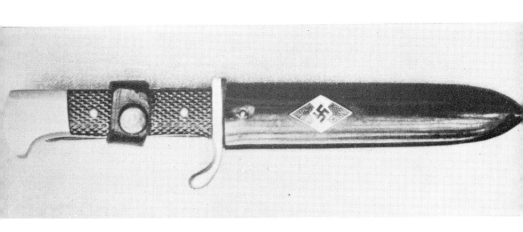

ABOVE: Leader of the HJ Levante (Hungarian HJ), wearing the Fahrtenmesser, note the unusal ornation to the scabbard.

Library of Congress photo collection

LEFT: Unusual variation of the HJ Fahrtenmesser, thought to be either Russian or Bulgarian in origin, and worn by the pro-German youth units formed during the occupation of these areas. The hilt is particularly distinctive in having the cyrillic 'B' insetted in the face.

Weller & Dufty Ltd

DLV and NSFK

The DLV (Deutsche Luft-sportsverband—the German Airsports Association) was a para-military air training organisation run by the Nazi Party prior to official rearmament. The NSFK (National Soziali-stiches Flieger Korps — National Socialist Flying Corps) came about after the formation of the Luft-waffe, and replaced the DLV.

Members of the DLV, wearing the DLV knife, and the DLV dagger—this being the forerunner of the M1935 Luftwaffe Flier's dagger, the DLV knife pattern being used, modified, by the NSFK when this organisation came into being.

Photo Colonel C. M. Dodkins collection

The German Air Sports Leader's dagger, Model 1933. This dagger the style of which is the forerunner to the Luftwaffe Model 1935, was one of the first militarised trappings of an organisation which, under the guise of being a civilian air sports organisation, provided a backbone of trained flying and ground crew personnel on the creation of the Luftwaffe. The metal fittings of the hilt are of silver-plated brass casting, bearing the sunwheel swastika in the pommel and quillon block. The grip is wood, and wrapped in blue leather, and the blade is long, straight, unfullered and pointed. The scabbard is solid leather, devoid of any inner liner, and bears silver-plated fittings. Compared to the later Luftwaffe version, the DLV Leader's dagger displays a rather crude mode of construction, the grip being manufactured without a wire wrap, and the pommel being flat, as against concave, and secured to the blade by the peening over of the tang. This version of the DLV dagger is rather scarce, as it was superseded in 1934 by a second pattern, which was of more professional construction, having die-cast fittings, and a screw threaded tang and pommel, this being easily disassembled. Apart from the utilisation of the solid leather scabbard, it was indistinguishable from the Luftwaffe patterns with the steel lined, leather wrapped scabbard.

Photo courtesy Charles Scaglioni

ABOVE: A scarce miniature DLV dagger, in the style of the Leader's Model 1935, bearing on the blade the inscription *Dem Kampfer fur Deutsche Luftfahrt Fliegeruntergruppe Berlin* ('The fighters for the German Air Service, Berlin Secondary Air Group). Like the second type, Model 1935 dagger, this piece can be dismantled, and it is extremely well made. However, due to its diminutive size, it is doubtful if it had a scabbard with suspension chains, or if it was ever worn as a dagger at all. Most probably it was a privately (ie, non official) manufactured item, given as a token to distinguished members of the DLV who had laboured to ease the formation of the Luftwaffe, and provide it with a cadre of trained leader personnel. Blade length 7 inches.

Wallis and Wallis

ABOVE: Presentation DLV officer's dagger, second model. Engraved on the reverse of the upper scabbard chape: *Dem Förderer des Deutschen Luftsports, Herrn Dir. P. Speck Luftsports, Ostgruppe Berlin VI, 1936* ('To the furtherance of German Airsports, Director P. Speck, Airsports, Ostgruppe Berlin VI, 1936').

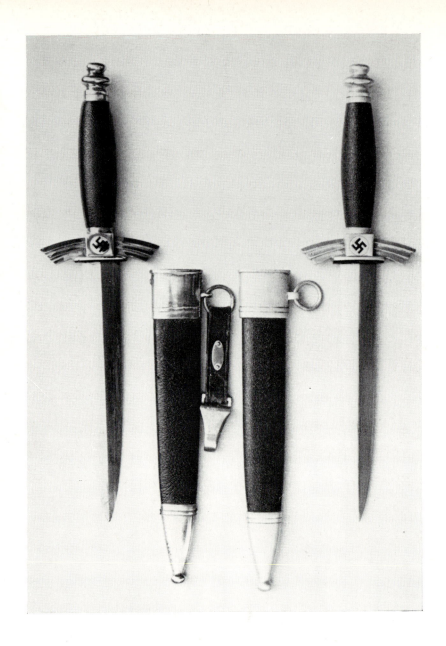

On the left is the DLV Flier's knife, silver-plated hilt fittings, with dark blue leather grip wrap, and blue leather scabbard.

On the right is the NSFK version of the Flier's knife (introduced 1937), identical in form to the DLV pattern, with the distinction of being made with die-cast aluminium fittings, and blue crackled enamel finish to the scabbard. Blade lengths $6\frac{1}{2}$ inches.

RAD (Reichs Arbeitsdienst- Reich Labour Service)

The RAD hewer was introduced early in 1934, for service wear by all personnel of the Labour Service.

The hewer is a distinctive accoutrement to the uniform, having a heavy steel hilt with silver or nickel finish. The blade is broad and falchion in style, bearing on the obverse the etched motto *Arbeit Adelt* ('Labour Ennobles'). The scabbard is a broad steel body with black stove enamelled finish and silvered fittings, the lower section displaying the RAD emblem.

The hewer was worn suspended from a leather belt loop, to which there was stitched a fitting clasp housing a spring-loaded catch, which mated with the loop situated on the locket of the scabbard.

The hewer first introduced in 1934 bore an unusual distinction, that being the stag horn grips covering totally the surface area of the handle. In 1936, this design was slightly modified, to having the projecting 'beak' of the pommel cleared of the stag horn grip. Illustrated right are 1934 and 1936 variations of the hewer, and below a 1936 hewer pattern with original belt suspension loop. Blade length: 9¾ inches.

A third variation to the hewer was manufactured, seemingly in wartime. This version is quite distinctive in having a fatter type blade, with the etched motto situated on the blade reverse.

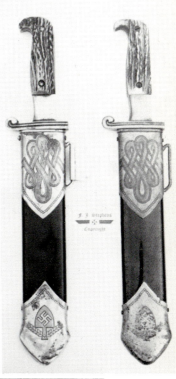

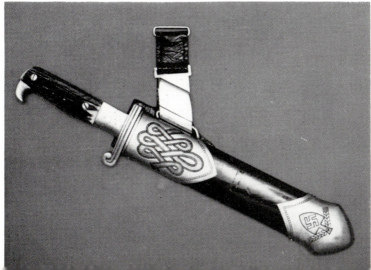

ABOVE: Hitler being greeted by RAD Leader Konstantin Hierl. Note Hierl's dagger, with the distinctive feature of being a twin strap Model 1934. Prior to the introduction of the M1937, Hierl wore the basic dagger with the regular type strap. However, after 1937 when the Leader's Dagger became authorised, the RAD Leader continued to wear his basic model, but had the leather straps fitted to the special modification on the scabbard.

OPPOSITE, TOP: The RAD hewer in wear.

Both photos courtesy Steve Bloomer

OPPOSITE PAGE:

LOWER: Highly unusual RAD hewer variation. Although basic in construction, this dagger features the most odd fitment of having a TeNo blade, evidenced by the distinctive shape of the Technical Corps blade, and the inclusion on the reverse of the original TeNo ordnance eagle, and the manufacturer's trade-mark. The obverse of the blade is etched with the RAD motto. The dagger is totally original in construction (although the bolts in the grip are non-contemporary), and seemingly the only logical explanation to the existence of such an unusual variation is that it was a factory error. Most probably a TeNo blade was inadvertently etched and finished for fitment to an RAD hilt. Normal inspection procedures should have detected this item and condemned it from passing out of the factory, however, it appears that this example missed detection.

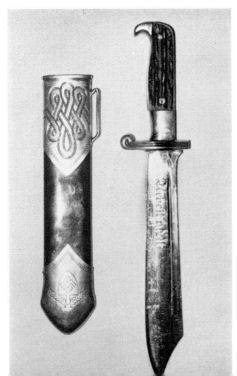

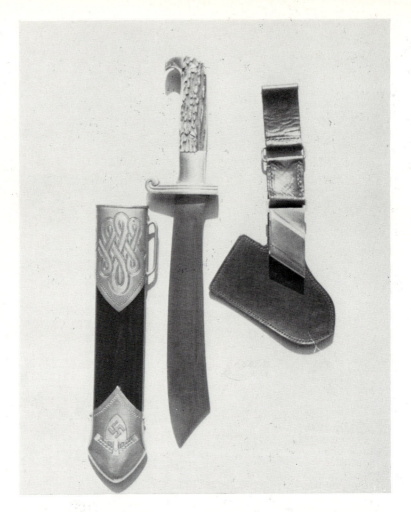

Another unusual non-official variation RAD hewer, totally basic and original in construction, but being completely devoid of blade motto. Close examination of the blade gave no indication of there ever having been a motto and subsequently having been polished out, so it must be presumed that this, like the previous item, is a factory error.

F. G. Wells collection

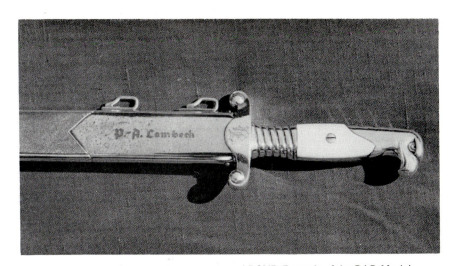

ABOVE: Example of the RAD Model 1937, having been personalised by the late owner. The back of the scabbard is engraved with the name P. A. Lambech, and the reverse of the crossguard is also ornamented with a motif of these initials.

John Burden collection

For colour illustration of RAD Leader's Model 1937 dagger, see page 41.

LEFT: Variation RAD Leader's dagger, shown with a basic Model 1937. Two features make this example distinctive from the basic model; the securing screw situated on the face grip, and the eagle and swastika RAD device on the crossguard. At the time of writing no contemporary reference to this variation has been located.

Walt Nichols collection

Reichsarbeitsführer Hierl in Bulgaria. Members of the RAD delegation on this visit to Bulgaria in 1938 were all presented with a Bulgarian dagger by their hosts, the RAD Leader is seen wearing his example.

*RAD Yearbook,
1938*

TeNo
(Technische Nothilfe, Technical Emergency Corps)

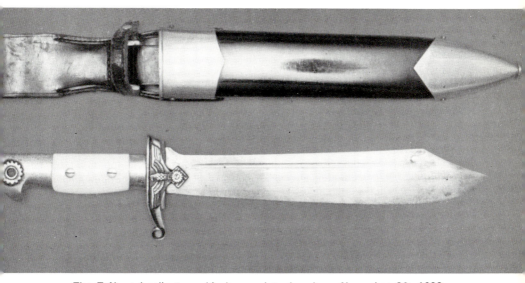

The TeNo subordinate rank's hewer, introduced on November 30, 1938. The sole manufacturer of the TeNo contract was the firm of Carl Eickhorn, of Solingen, whose mark, together with the TN inspection mark, appears on the blade. Each piece was numbered for issue, the number appearing on the blade underneath the obverse langent and also on the upper lip of the scabbard throat.

The hilt is constructed of a cast alloy, bearing the TeNo cogwheel device in the pommel, and the TeNo eagle and swastika emblem on the crossguard, and is finished in nickel-plate. Two white celluloid slab grips are fitted, each marked on the inside with the Eickhorn trademark, and fitted in position by means of two countersunk bolts.

This hewer was worn by all ranks from Nothelfer to Hauptscharführer. It was suspended from the belt by means of a black leather frog, which had a metal spring clip attachment to the frog loop on the back of the scabbard. A variation which had the belt loop permanently riveted to the scabbard frog loop is also known to exist.

Two patterns of knot were worn with the hewer. A silver and purple acorn with red and purple stem, and silver cord with four purple stripes was worn by TeNo non-commissioned leaders on air raid duty. The other version had a silver acorn with purple top and orange stem, and a silver cord with two purple stripes. It was worn by TeNo personnel on stand-by service.

For TeNo senior officer's dagger, see colour plate on page 44.

RLB

Note: (RLB Reichs Luftschutz-
bund) was the German Air
Defence Organisation roughly
equivalent to the British ARP of
the same period.

RLB sunburst emblem as used
prior to 1938.

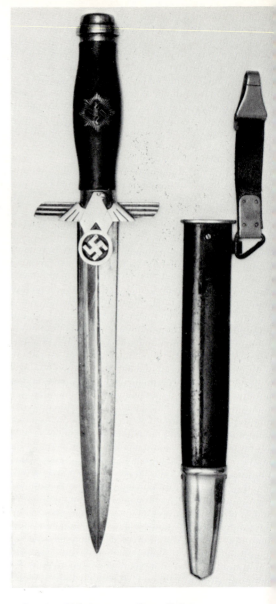

Introduced in 1936, the NCO dagger for the RLB has cast brass fittings,
with nickel-plate finish. The grip is ebony, and bears the sunburst emblem
of the RLB with a swastika device situated in the lower section. The scabbard is pressed steel, with nickel-plate fittings, and the dagger was worn
suspended from a black leather belt loop. In 1938, the dagger pattern was
slightly modified, having the RLB grip emblem replaced with a sunburst
bearing a large dark blue enamel swastika.

ABOVE: RLB officer (on right) assisting in a street collection on behalf of the Winter Help Organisation, Berlin, 1939. He is wearing the RLB leader's dagger as shown in the colour plate on page 45. The longer blade length and domed pommel (compared to the NCO dagger) can be seen even in this view.

DRK (Deutsches Rotes Kreuz, German Red Cross)

The DRK enlisted personnel hewing knife, designed as both a dress item and service uniform accoutrement. The crossguard and pommel are cast zinc anodised with a dull silver finish. The grips are black checkered plastic, on the face, and a smooth face black plastic on the reverse. The crossguard langet bears the device of the DRK, and the reverse langet is plain, though in

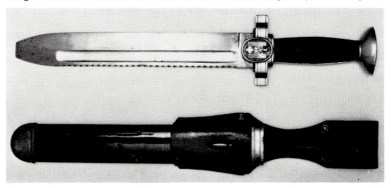

many cases it is sometimes encountered with an issue number stamped into it. The blade is broad, serrated, and square tipped. It is designed to serve as a utility tool for the manufacturing of splints, etc. The scabbard is steel, stove enamelled black, and with silver-anodised steel fittings. Suspension is by means of a black leather, bayonet-type frog. When worn on dress occasions, a blue and silver portepee was worn. Blade length: 10½ inches.

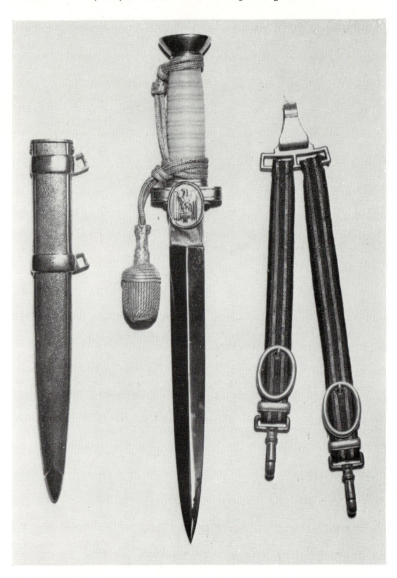

DRK officer's dagger. The hilt fittings of this piece are made of cast zinc, with nickel-plate finish. The grip is solid celluloid, and colour variations ranging from pure white to deep orange are encountered. The blade is straight, highly polished and pointed, with a pronounced central spine, and the scabbard is steel, with a nickel-plate, and stipple finish to the central face areas. The example illustrated is complete with original silver portepee. The suspension straps, as illustrated, have an aluminium facing with red stripes. Members of the social welfare service also wore the DRK dagger, but distinguished themselves by the wearing of suspension straps with a dull aluminium facing with purple stripes, on a grey velvet backing, and square buckles—quite distinctive to the oval DRK buckles as shown. Blade length: $9\frac{3}{4}$ inches.

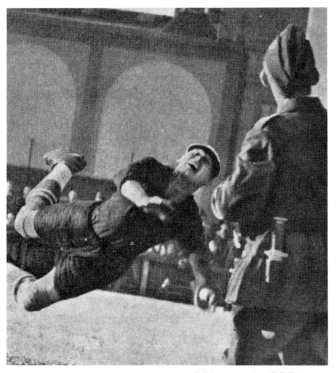

A DRK official on duty at a sportsfield, note the DRK hewer being worn. *SWF photo*

RIGHT: An example of the DRK Führerdolch (leader's dagger) showing basic manufacturing variations. Note the square-holed scabbard bands (round-holed were also found) and the dark coloured (orange) hilt. The dagger shown opposite has by contrast a white hilt and more rounded edges to the scabbard bands.

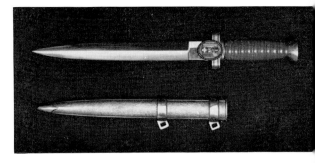

A rare example of a presentation DRK officer's dagger, with etched blade. Such pieces were not solely presented to DRK Officials, but also to selected dignitaries who had rendered some support, or valuable service to the efficient operation of the DRK. Among those who received such awards were, it is believed, Field-Marshal Erwin Rommel, and the Swiss born SS Officer Leonardi Conti, who committed suicide whilst in prison during the Nuremburg trials. The example illustrated is named for Dr. Georg Siemans, and on the blade reverse is etched *'Dankbarre der Führer'* with a facsimile of Hitler's signature placed on the reverse langet.

Robert McCarthy collection

Polizei and Feuerwehr
(Police and Fire Department)

Police dress bayonet, introduced prior to the formation of the Third Reich, but retained for wear during the early years.

The hilt is made of cast brass, ornamented with an eagle's head pommel, and nickel-plated. Twin stag horn grips are riveted to the tang, and bear the insetted emblem of a Weimarian eagle within a sunburst. The upswept quillon is decorated with a continuation of oak leaves, and a down-turned shellguard projects over the blade. Black leather scabbard with nickel fittings. Blade length: $9\frac{3}{4}$ inches.

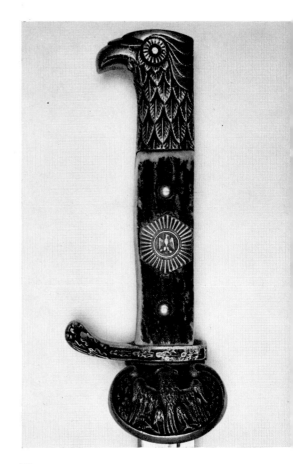

Members of the Feldjager taking the oath of loyalty. Personnel of this unit wore the basic Weimarian type police bayonet, distinguished only in having a newly designed badge indicative of the National Socialist government, this showing a flighted eagle with the swastika on the breast, and clutching a sword and lightning bolts.

Göring collection,
Library of Congress

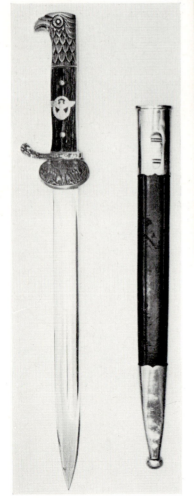

German Police bayonet, circa 1935. Basically a Weimarian bayonet, but having the German Police emblem mounted on the grip.

H. Haslem collection

80

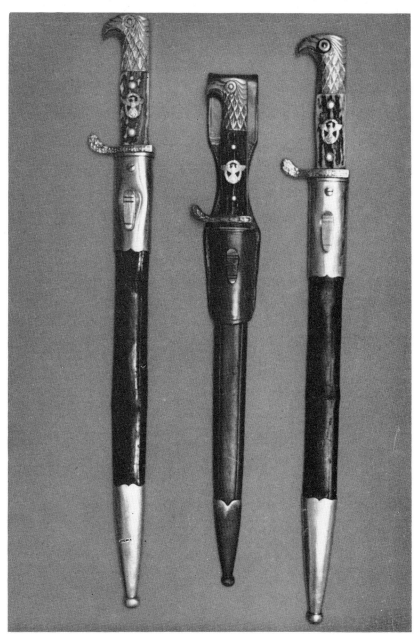

German Police bayonets, introduced for all police personnel as from 1935. Two scabbard finishes are encountered, black leather for Gendarme Police, and brown leather for Metropolitan. Shown left to right: Long pattern without bayonet mortice; short pattern lightweight version, having aluminium hilt; long pattern with bayonet mortice slot. Blade lengths $9\frac{3}{4}$ inches and $7\frac{7}{8}$ inches.

Dagger of the Water Protection Police Service. Identical in style to the Naval dirk, with the pre-1938 pommel, the Water Protection Police dirk differs in having a blue leather wrap to the grip. Some of the earlier examples produced in 1938, bore the distinguishing feature of having the Police eagle and swastika device (as seen on swords and bayonets) fitted to the grip, though this was not a very common variation. After 1939, members of the Water Protection Police became authorised to wear, if desired, the Police sword. The dagger was worn suspended from gilt braid straps with purple stripes, and army type oval buckles, with a gold and purple knot.

F. Featherstone collection

 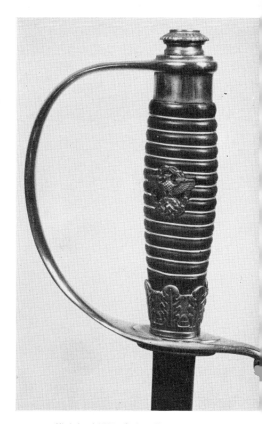

Swords for wear by Police and Fire Department officials. LEFT: Subordinate rank's Degen sword. RIGHT: Leader rank's sword. Both patterns have a black wood grip with police emblem insetted. The overall finish to the hilt is nickel-plate, and the swords were carried in a black steel scabbard.

Major John R. Angolia collection

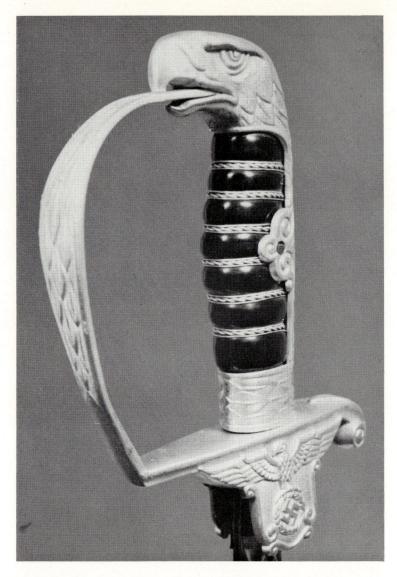

Sword for the Justice Official. Two variations of this sword exist, silver finish for Prison Administration, and gilt finish for Justices. The hilt is finely styled in the form of an eagle's head, with the eagle and swastika displayed on both the obverse and reverse langet. Scabbard is black stove enamelled steel. As an alternative to the sword, Justice and Prison Officials could wear the State Official's dagger, in either gilt or silver finish.

Major John R. Angolia collection

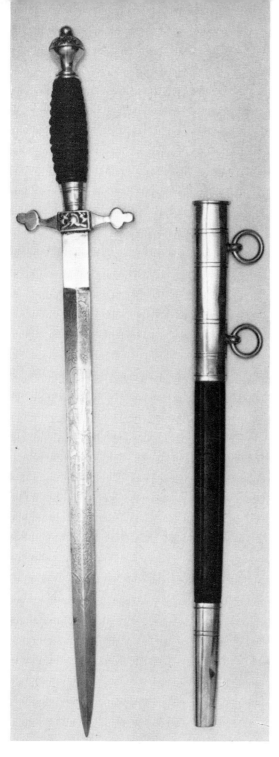

LEFT: Fire Department senior official's dagger. Two patterns exist, these being silver (or nickel) finish, and gold finish for higher ranks. The grip is made of wood with a black leather wrap, the crossguard being ornated with the Fire Department helmet and crossed axes. The blade is etched on both sides with foliage, and fire department emblems. The dagger is carried in a black leather scabbard, with nickel (or silver) plated fittings, and suspended by twin leather straps. A variation having a single strap suspension was manufactured.

NEXT PAGE: Variation Fire Department dagger having white ivory grip, gilt fittings, and contained in a black stove enamelled scabbard, with single ring suspension. The dagger pattern was commonly encountered during the pre-Nazi period of the Weimarian republic, it was however, continued in service during the Third Reich by those officials who preferred to continue the wearing of their pre-Nazi period dagger. Both sides of the weapon are shown.

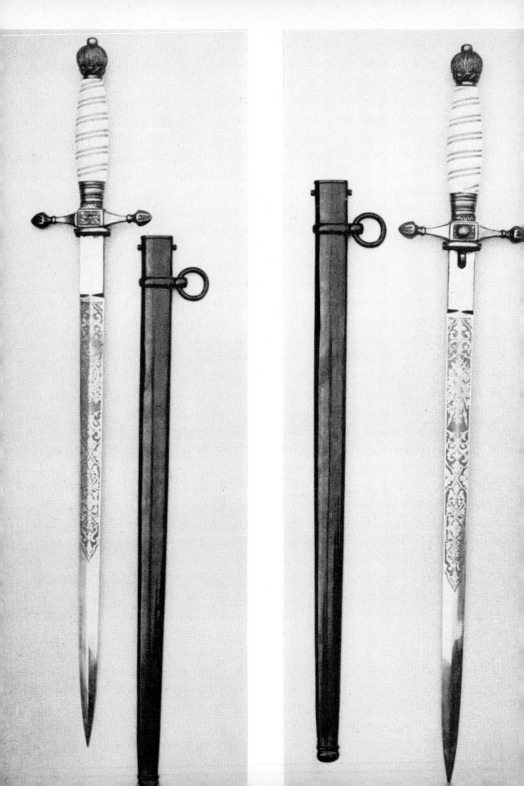

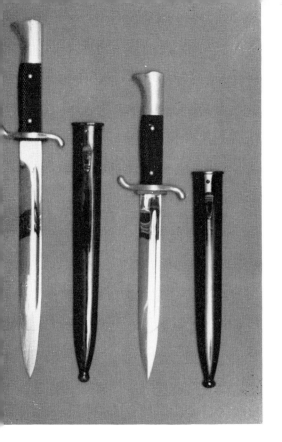

Sidearms for Fire Dept. personnel. Available in two lengths, $9\frac{7}{8}$ inches and $7\frac{7}{8}$ inches, with or without saw back blade. Hilts are cast alloy with bright nickel finish.

BELOW: Dress Axes for Fire Officials. De luxe versions have nickel-plate or gilt finish, fully etched with floral designs and Fire Service motifs. Standard issue dress axes have plain nickel-plate finish.
Eickhorn Kundendienst.

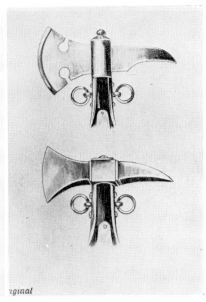

Railway and Waterway Protection Services

RIGHT: The Model 1935 Bahnschutz dagger, identical in style to the M1935 Army dagger, but having the distinctive feature of a purple/black celluloid grip. Metal fittings of the dagger are in silver plate finish.

John Burden collection

BELOW: Rare example of the Canals and Waterways Protection Service dagger. The dagger is constructed of die-cast aluminium, having a swastika placed on the upper face of the pommel, and the Army type crossguard and scabbard, distinguished by the horizontally grooved suspension bands. Like the model 1935, and the Army M1935, the blade length was the standard $10\frac{1}{4}$ inches. The grip, however, is distinctive, being the purple/black celluloid type. The straps of the dagger are black leather, with oval buckles. The example illustrated is in silver finish; it is believed that a gilt finish example exists.

F. G. Wells collection

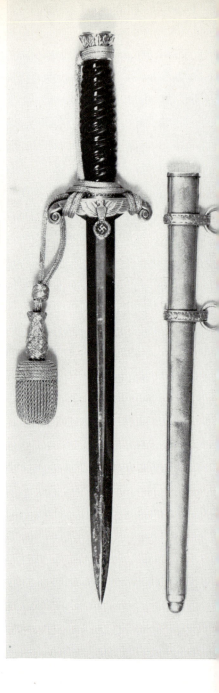

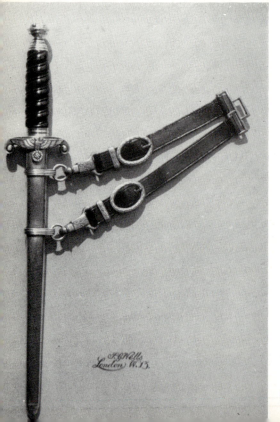

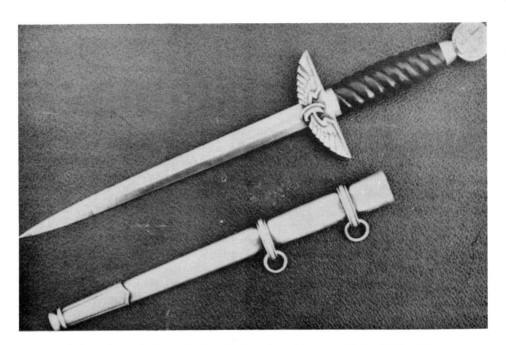

Railway Leader's dagger, believed to have been introduced during 1941, which was placed into a very limited production. All metal fitments were gilded, the pommel being ornamented with the curved arm swastika, and a swept wing Bahnschutz emblem placed on the crossguard. The grip is dark purple/black plastic. No other details are known. Actual weapon is shown above with a detailed drawing below.

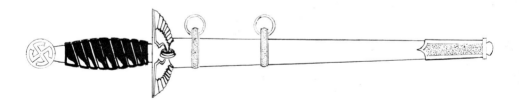

For the Model 1938 Railway Leader's dagger, see colour plate on page 37.

Postal Protection Service

Introduced in 1939 for wear by officials serving in the Postschutz, the leader's dagger is a very rare standard issue model, all of which appear to have been manufactured by the concern of Paul Weyersberg, Solingen. What is somewhat more interesting than the basic rarity of this dagger is, strangely, the unusual number of variations that exist to the basic model. The standard pattern illustrated here, is as follows: Cast brass hilt fittings, with nickel finish. The grip is ebony, and bears the eagle and swastika with lightning bolts device. The crossguard forms a stylised eagle's head with outspread wings, bearing the swastika on the face, usually marked on the quillon underside with DRP – – – (number). The scabbard is sheet steel, stove enamelled black, and with brass fittings nickel-plated, and suspended with chains not unlike those utilised on the M1934 Luftwaffe dagger. Blade length 9½ inches.

Known variations have been listed to date:

As above, but having the grip emblem inlaid in the surface of the wood.

As above, yet having the grip emblem mounted on the grip surface.

As above, but without any DRP markings.

As above, without markings, no insignia fitted in or to the grip, and with a leather finish to the scabbard.

A short pattern having 7½ inch blade is recorded, with leather wrap to the grip with surface mounted emblem, contained in a short steel scabbard with single suspension ring. This latter item has been identified as being the Postschutz Man's dagger, yet there is no evidence to support this view, except the unusual size of the dagger. It is more likely that this is, yet again, a more extreme variation of the leader's dagger, and that the Postschutz Man's dagger *per se* is a doubtful classification.

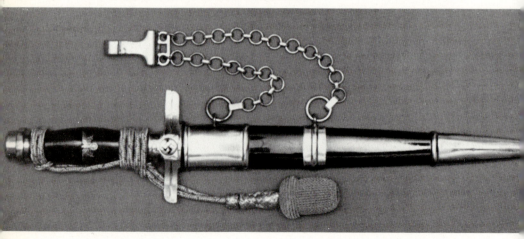

OPPOSITE PAGE:

Presentation Postschutz dagger. This rare variation is a privately presented piece, and has solid silver fittings ornated with scroll and oak leaf designs. The blade is damascus steel, large rose pattern, and bears on the obverse 'From the Postschutz of the district of Erfurt', and on the reverse of the blade 'Truth is the Mark of Honour'. The chain suspension illustrated is incorrect, and a later addition. *Courtesy J. A. Morrison collection*

Zoll
(Customs Service)

BELOW: The dagger for the Land Customs and Sea Customs, as well as for officials of the Ministry of Finance, was introduced in August, 1937. For Landzoll the dagger was finished in either satin aluminium or silver plate on steel, with green leather wrap to the grip and scabbard, for Wasserzoll a gold finish with blue leather wrap was utilised.

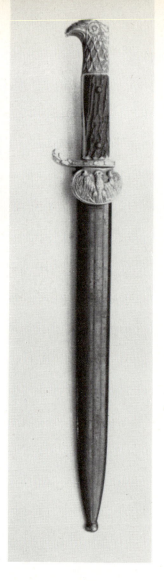

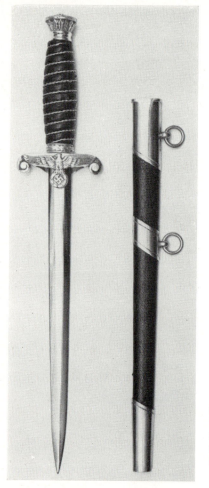

ABOVE: Customs dress bayonet, gilt finish over brass with stag horn grips. The illustrated item is contained in a black stove enamelled steel scabbard.

Wallis and Wallis

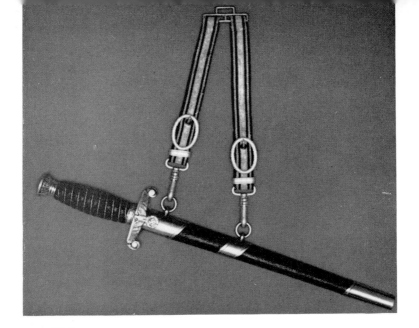

ABOVE: Land Customs dagger shown with original straps, silver braid with twin green stripes, sewn on to a green velvet background. Sea Customs were issued with blue braid straps with gilt fittings. The portepee knot, where worn was for Landzoll, in the standard Wehrmacht type silver aluminium cord, and for Wasserzoll it is thought to be a gold aluminium cord knot.

LEFT: Variation on the customs bayonet having a leather and brass scabbard, identical to the short police pattern. A further variation is shown in the *Eickhorn Kundendienst,* having the same basic configuration with leather scabbard, but without the shell guard as illustrated.

Private collection

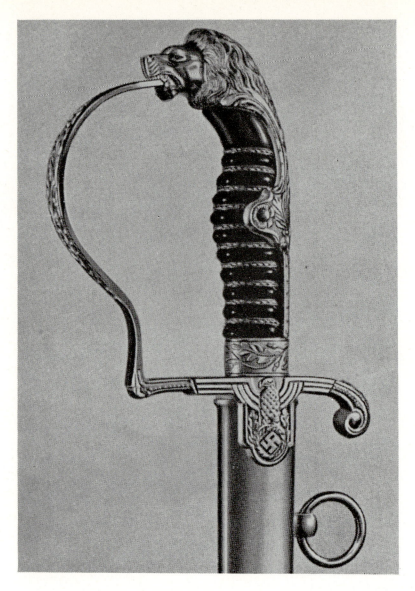

Sword pattern carried by Wasserzoll officials, having lion head pommel, ornate back strap and knucklebow, and the eagle and swastika on the crossguard. The scabbard is black leather with gilt fittings.

Eickhorn Kundendienst

Land Customs officers, wearing both the old and new pattern uniforms. Seen in wear is the silver finish plain hilt Sabel.

Photo Hugh Page Taylor collection

Forestry Service
(Forstbeamte)

RIGHT: Third Reich period Forestry Cutlass of unidentified manufacture. The hilt fittings of this piece are aluminium, with gilt finish, the grips are stag horn with gilt acorn device mounted on the surface. The blade is particularly interesting, in having a proof mark and an extended fuller projecting through the tip. The blade is etched with hunting scenes. The scabbard is black leather, with engraved brass mounts.

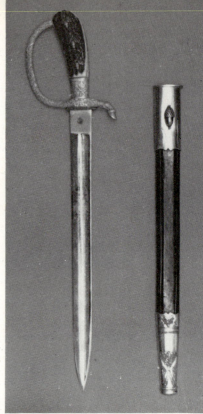

LEFT: Two variations of hunting cutlass, for Official and Senior Official of the Forestry service. Illustration detailed from the Klaas catalogue, 1939.

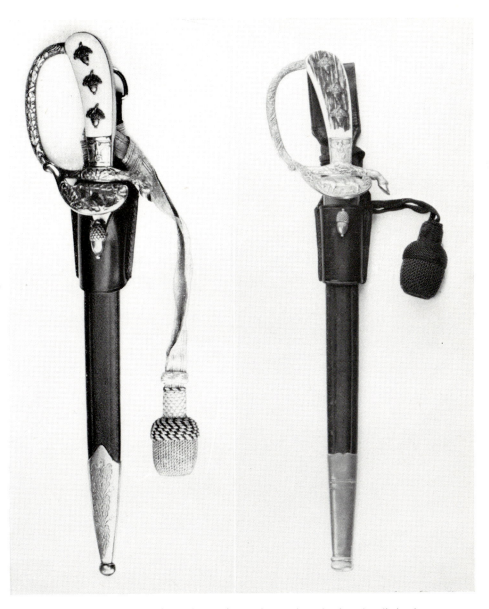

Two rare variations of the Forester's hunting cutlass, having the distinctive design of the eagle and swastika cast into the grip ferrule. The Senior model on the left has white ivory grips, and the lower ranks on the right has stag horn. The scabbards are, on the left, green leather with gilt fittings, and black leather with gilt fittings.

Wallis and Wallis

Hunting Association
(Reichsbund Deutsche Jägerschaft)

A rare Hunting Association sword presented to Göring, when serving in his capacity of *Reichsjägermeister.*

The hilt of this piece is finely chiselled steel, portraying a wolf on the pommel, surmounting a grip stylised with hunting ornaments over a foliage design background. The quillons are in the form of hoofs, and the blade etched with the inscription *Dem Reichsjägermeister.*

Wallis and Wallis

BELOW: Hunting cutlasses, having stag horn grip bearing acorn mounts on the face. They were introduced in 1936 for wear by all members of the RDJ. The hilt fittings are in silver or nickel-plate, and the blades are finely etched on both sides with hunting scenes.

Eickhorn Kundendienst

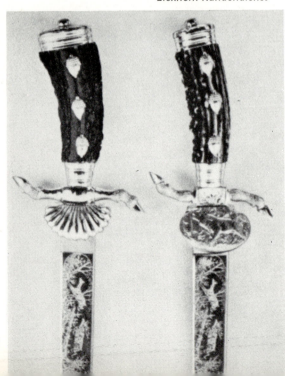

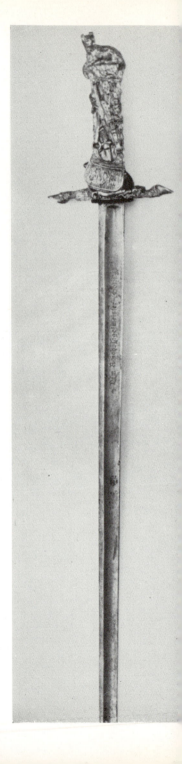

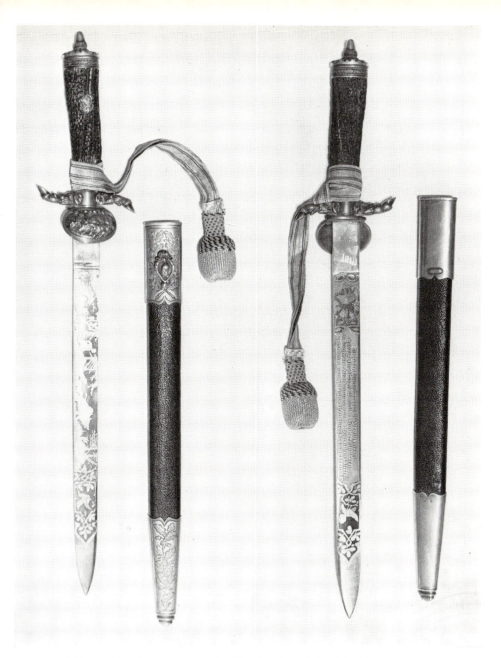

A fine and handsome presentation Hunting Association hirschfanger, manufactured by the Holler company. The obverse of the blade is a standard pattern etch, but the reverse bears a presentation inscription from the Kaiserlauten Hunting Association. The scabbard is fine green morocco leather, with silvered fittings engraved with oak leaf designs.

Private collection

ABOVE: Göring at a political training school, wearing the von Rosen dagger.

US Army photo
from captured German newsreel film

LEFT: One of Göring's favourite daggers, a wedding gift from his brother-in-law Count Erik von Rosen. The knife was manufactured from a pattern that von Rosen's wife gave to her husband, commemorating his famous transcontinental flight from South to North Africa. Von Rosen presented this piece to Göring; the dagger has a bronze hilt with silver highlights, and is inscribed in runic on the guard 'A knife from Erik to Hermann'. The scabbard is inlaid with red leather, and bears the markings on the side of the craftsman Borgila, of Sweden.

Photo courtesy West Point Museum collection

One of Göring's Hunting daggers captured along with his possessions, and 'purchased' works of art from the famous 'Aladdin's Cave' haul at Konigsee. This choice dagger has a fluted ivory grip, with gilt hilt fittings inset with tourmelains and semi-precious stones. The gilt finish scabbard has a hunting scene silhouetted over a green leather backing. The dagger was worn in a vertical configuration from a double chain suspension device. Since its capture, and after being inventoried and photographed in 1946, the dagger has disappeared.

Photograph by T. S. Law

Göring at a hunt meeting views the day's kill.

Göring collection,
Library of Congress

Göring's hunting dagger, shown in wear in the photograph, displayed alongside his signet ring.

Chris Farlowe photo
collection

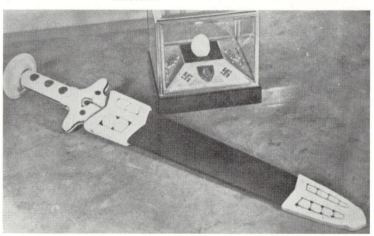

German Rifle Association

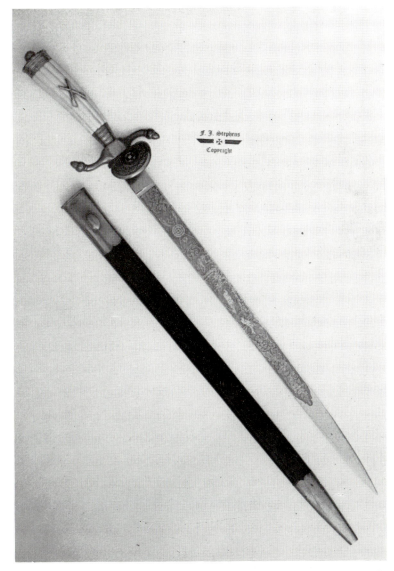

The hilt fittings of this cutlass are in nickel-plate, with a white celluloid grip bearing crossed rifles insignia. The projecting shell guard bears an oak leaf design, with the insetted emblem of the National Association. The blade is fully etched on both sides with targets and wildlife scenes. The scabbard is black leather with nickel fittings. A variation in the blade etching is recorded, having crossed epee and rifle with a stag's head design, this pattern is however, relatively rare. Blade length 15½ inches.

Mining Association
(Bergban)

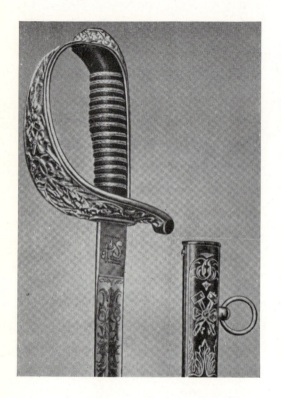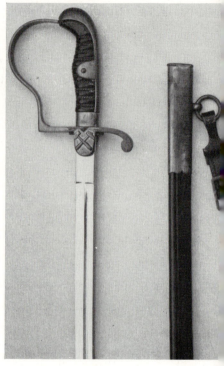

Two patterns of the Mining Official's sword.
LEFT: De-luxe variation of the Mining sword, having a half-basket ornated with floral motifs and the mining emblem.

Eickhorn Kundendienst

RIGHT: Plain gilt hilt with the crossed hammers of the service. The scabbard is black leather with gilt steel fittings.

Eric Campion collection

NPEA

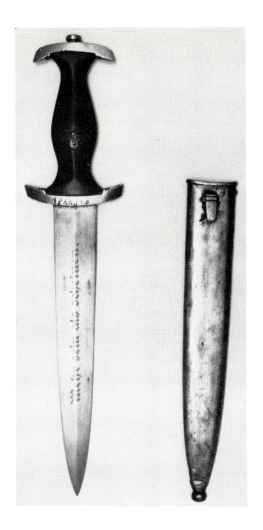

NPEA student's dagger. Introduced in 1935, the Student's Dagger carries the same styling as the political organisation daggers. The grip, however, for the lower ranks is devoid of insignia. The blade is etched with the motto *Mehr sein als scheinen* ('Be more than you appear to be'). The scabbard is of a bayonet type pattern, requiring a leather frog for suspension, and finished in an olive drab colour. NPEA Staff Leaders wore the basic NPEA dagger, having in the grip an inset party emblem. The scabbard pattern could be either the basic bayonet type, or the SA/SS version, having single ring suspension, and finished in either SA brown or SS black.

The example illustrated, has the unusual addition in the grip of a Flemish Nazi 'Der Vlaag' insignia, which although not a correct variation is contemporary to the manufacture of the piece, and was most probably unofficially added by the original owner.

NPEA Student and Staff Leader daggers, showing both the plain grip and the eagle inlay patterns.

The dagger shown left bears the distributor trade-mark of Karl Burgsmuller, of Charlottenburg, Berlin—the most commonly encountered trade-mark. The item right, is of Eickhorn manufacture, distinguished not only by the trade-mark, but also the formation of the blade motto; note the usuage of the long 's' at the beginning of the second and fourth words. The scabbard for this item (not shown) is the basic bayonet type, but this again differed from the Burgsmuller pattern, in that the interior springs of the scabbard were secured by a single screw mounted on the face of the scabbard above the frog stud, on the Burgsmuller pattern two screws, situated on the side of the scabbard, slightly to the back, are always encountered.

Frank Featherstone collection

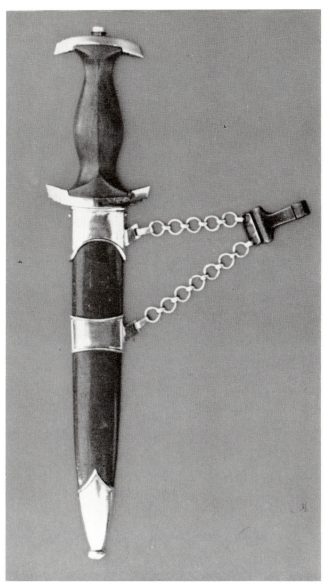

NPEA leader's dagger, Model 1936. Distinguished by the central mount on the scabbard, and the chain suspension, this pattern constitutes the rarest of the NPEA basic variations. The example shown has the plain grip, it is difficult to account for this, as the inlaid insignia should always be found with this version—possibly wartime restrictions forbade the usage of the grip inlay. A second recognised variation to the chained leader's dagger exists, thought to be an earlier model. This has a thinner centre scabbard mount, with swivel rings for chain attachment, rather than the fixed mounts on the later patterns.

Diplomatic Service

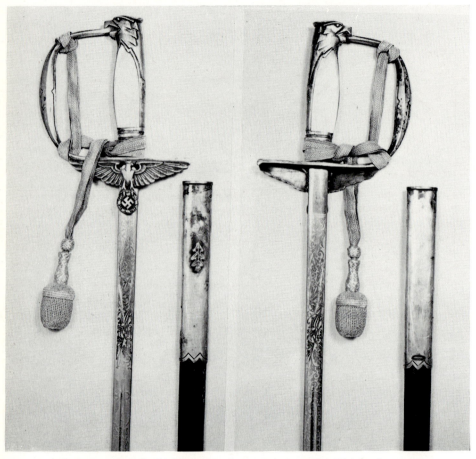

A fine example of the highly rare, and extremely beautiful, Diplomatic sword. Introduced in 1938, the sword appears to have been manufactured by only two firms, those of Carl Eickhorn, and Alcoso.

The whole of the metal portions of the hilt are silver-plated, having a pommel stylised in the form of an eagle's head, and with the Diplomatic eagle and swastika on the crossguard. The grips are made of simulated mother-of-pearl. The blade is straight and finely etched, bearing a foliage design and, on the obverse is the Diplomatic eagle and swastika. A short fuller, centrally placed, is also featured on the blade. The scabbard is made of fine blue morocco leather, with silver-plated mounts.

Shown attached to the above example, is the original *portepee*, a broad aluminium braid strap, with bulbous aluminium acorn.

Photo courtesy Charles Scaglioni

Diplomatic Officer's Dagger (on right), and the State Official's Dagger (left). The daggers for these two branches of the German Civil Service are identical in style, with the exception of one minor modification, that being the eagle's head on the crossguard. On the State Official's Dagger this faces towards the dexter (viz, same direction as on the pommel), but on the Diplomatic dagger it faces sinister —towards the back.

The dagger hilt is cast brass, the pommel ornated in the form of a stylised eagle's head, with inset simulated mother-of-pearl grips. The metal fittings of the dagger are silver-plated. The scabbard is steel, with stippled finish to the scabbard body, and suspension bands not unlike the Naval Officer's dirk pattern. The scabbard finish is silver, with a dark anodising to the recessed areas, the blade is plain, 10¼ inches in length. Senior Officials of both the Diplomatic Service and the State Officials Service wore their respective daggers with gold plate finish. The dagger was worn suspended from broad silver braid straps, with silver (or gold) finish square buckles.

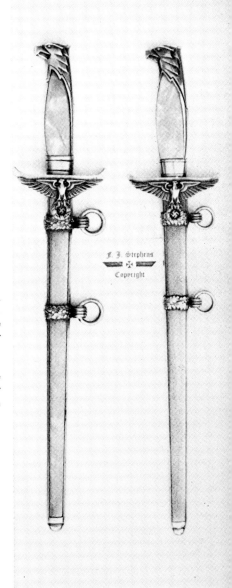

F. J. Stephens
Copyright

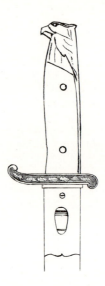

Dress Bayonet designed for wear by subordinate officials in the Diplomatic Service. Based on an illustration in the Alexander Coppel sales catalogue 1940.

Dagger for officials in the Eastern Territories. A dagger pattern that is believed to have been put into very limited production in 1941. The dagger is officially referred to in the period publication *Uniform-Markt,* 1940. Two contemporary references to the dagger exist, both of which carry an identical illustration to that reproduced here. No further details on the dagger are available.

Illustration courtesy Andrew Mollo

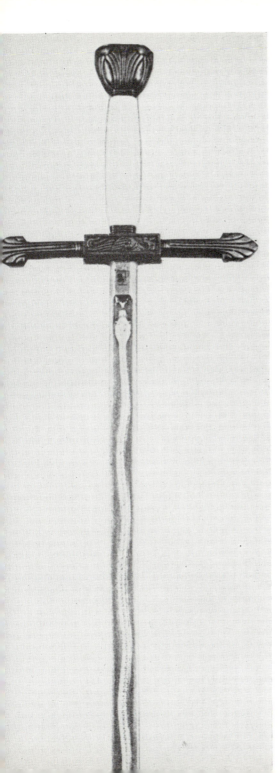

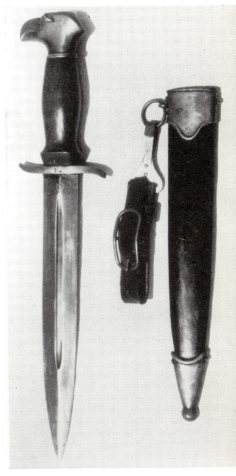

Unusual knife pattern, believed to be a non-official dagger pattern worn by recruited Nazi Party members in either Spain, or the Eastern Occupied Territories.

*Private collection,
photo by Marc Brown*

LEFT: Unidentified sword pattern, that was shown illustrated in the Eickhorn book, *Leisten und Dienen*.

Service and Dress Bayonets

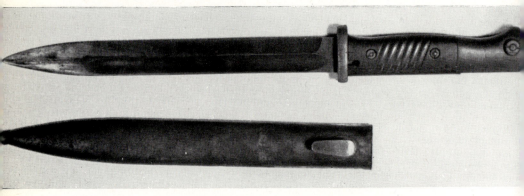

ABOVE: Mauser service bayonet, Model 84/98. The standard issue bayonet for all service troops in the German Armed forces, it was designed for use with the rifle pattern Gew 98 and Kar 98. The metal fittings are completely blued, with a preservative designed to halt rusting when carried on field duty. The scabbard is pressed steel, and the bayonet was worn suspended from a black leather frog.

BELOW: The extremely rare Model 1942 Kar bayonet. Introduced in 1942, this bayonet was put into limited production, and the main manufacturer of the piece appears to have been the Eickhorn concern. The hilt is particularly interesting, having contained within the grip a small utility knife, which folds and locks in the grip. In 1957, an almost exact copy of this bayonet pattern was produced for use on the AR 10 rifle which was issued to the Soudanese.

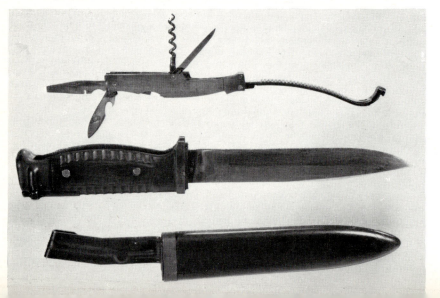

Dress Bayonets with de luxe etched blades

Virtually every manufacturer of blades in the Third Reich, produced as a de luxe optional extra, a series of variation blade etchings for dress bayonets. Thus, for the cost of a few extra marks, a purchaser could obtain ex-stock a basic dress bayonet which had additional refinements, such as stag horn grips, decorated pommel, and an etched blade. The cost of making an individual template for etching to each customer's requirements would have normally been beyond the pocket of the average purchaser. However, as such a de luxe extra to the basic pattern could be produced by the thousand once the template had been produced, the individual cost on a mass produced basis became very reasonable, and many soldiers added that little extra to their own personal property by paying the additional cost. The range of designs produced during the period is immense, many hundreds of combinations being known. For the more wealthy individual the blade bearing his own personal design, or dedication, extended the vast range of varieties and presentation pieces even further. The following de luxe patterns are displayed to show just some of the variations of blade etching that can be encountered Thanks are due to Jack Daniels of Gretna, Louisiana, who specialises in collecting etched blades, for making these pieces from his collection available.

ABOVE: Standard Eickhorn produced variation featuring Luftwaffe eagle and and aircraft, with the motto *Zur Erinnerung an meine Dienstzeit* ('In memory of my military service').

BELOW: Rare basic etching, produced very early during the Third Reich period, probably 1933 or 1934, featuring the standard service commemoration motto, but utilising a sans serif style of lettering—not popular in the Third Reich. Note also the off-centre grip studs, a characteristic commonly encountered during the Imperial and Weimarian periods, but replaced by the centrally situated style during 1933-45. No maker's mark.

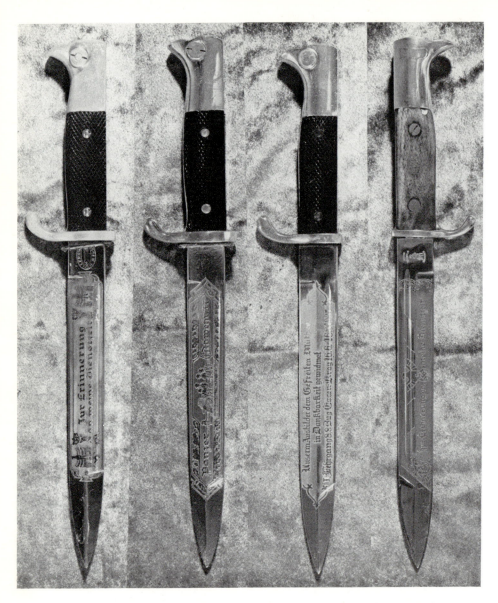

LEFT to RIGHT: F. W. Holler ex-stock pattern with Wehrmacht eagles and service legend; Eickhorn pattern, showing Panzer Abwehr etching; Eickhorn pattern with special purchase inscription, detailing the piece as a presentation in grateful recognition for service, dated 16.8.1937; Anton Winger variation, having wood grips—possibly a later addition—reverse of blade featuring eagle and swastika with service dedication.

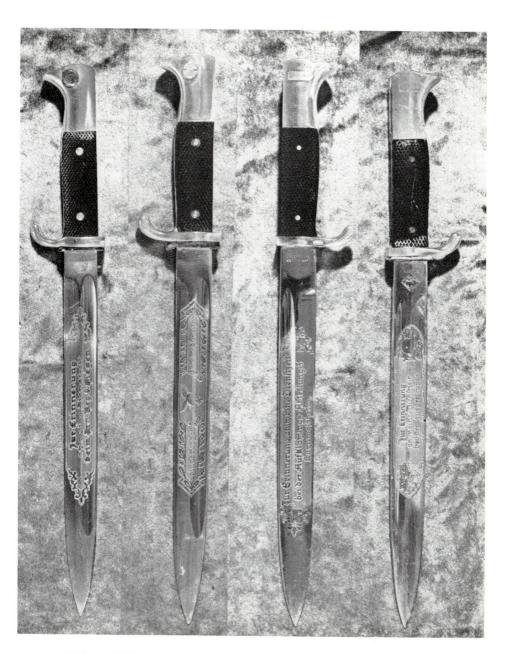

LEFT to RIGHT: Special Holler etching, commemorating military service in Regiment 9 Flying Section; Eickhorn basic with Luftwaffe style etching; special regimental etching pattern, manufactured by Hiller of Bad Cankstatt, commemorating service in Aufklarungs-Abteilung 5, at Kornwestheim; standard Puma pattern with etched pattern for service in flight section.

Obverse and reverse of a Seilheimer manufactured piece, showing standard service commemoration inscription, and on the reverse, Wehrmacht eagles with aircraft. The aircraft shown, Junkers 87A and Heinkel 51 suggest the 1936-37 period.

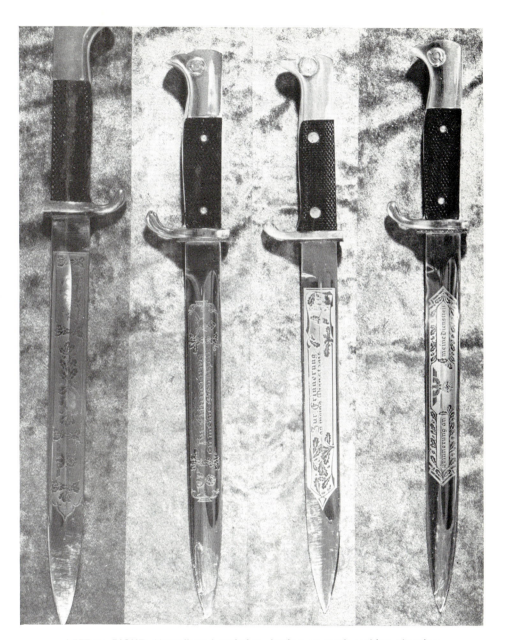

LEFT to RIGHT: Unattributed variation, having ex-stock etching showing gunners' oak leaves, and Army eagle and swastika; Paul Seilheimer ex-stock pattern having both Luftwaffe and Army eagle and swastika patterns; early Pack variation, note off-centre grip studs, and standard etch motto with biplane; Paul Seilheimer variation having eagle and swastika device in central section.

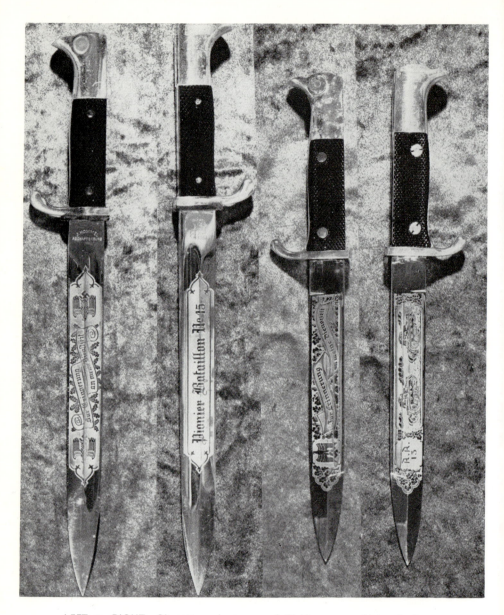

LEFT to RIGHT: Obverse and reverse of Eickhorn manufactured piece, bearing also military retailers marking (J. Hommel, Ashaffenburg), with ex-stock obverse etching, and *Pioneer Battalion No. 45* on reverse; unattributed early type carbine pattern dress bayonet (short $7\frac{7}{8}$ inch blade as against $9\frac{7}{8}$ inch for normal long pattern) with service motto on obverse, and tanks on reverse with *A.A. 13.*

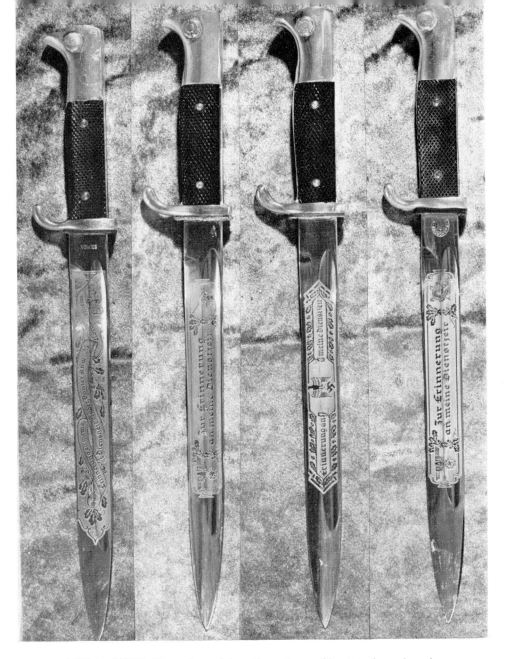

LEFT to RIGHT: Unusual special motto pattern, without trade-mark, only 'Solingen' marking, commemorating military service in Panzer Abwehr 25; ex-stock Paul Seilheimer pattern; unattributed piece, having Wehrmacht eagle within central panel surrounded by service motto; Holler manufactured piece, ex-stock with service motto.

LEFT and RIGHT: Stag horn grip de luxe patterns. Obverse and reverse of WKC pattern, bearing *Jäger Regiment 99* etching; Paul Seilheimer ex-stock pattern having Wehrmacht and Army eagle patterns with service motto, plus cavalry battle scene on reverse.

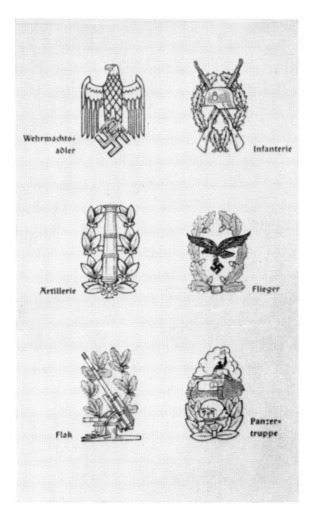

A manufacturer's selection of standard engravings for the pommel of the dress bayonet. Design ornamentations such as these were optional purchases for the recipient of the bayonet. As an alternative, personal motifs were sometimes engraved on the pommels.

Eickhorn Kundendienst

Knives and Miscellaneous Edged Pieces

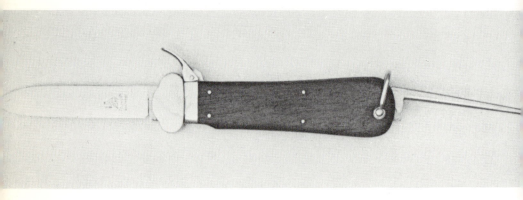

Gravity Blade Knife

The knife utilised by airborne troops in the German Air Force, and the Army who were responsible for paratroops during the early years of the Luftwaffe pre-1939. The knife is known as a gravity blade knife, determined by the feature of having the blade retained inside the grip by means of a pressure spring. It is released by suspending the pressure on the blade, holding the knife in a down position, and allowing the blade to be withdrawn from the interior by gravity. When the spring release was permitted to activate again, the blade was held retained in the projected position. The idea of this device, was to facilitate extraction and operation of the knife blade when the user might otherwise be hindered in having an arm tied (eg, entangled in a parachute harness if landing in a tree). Also fitted to the knife is a marlin spike, intended for use where a puncturing device is required. Two patterns of the gravity knife are known to exist, one being a solid built design, the other capable of being stripped down.

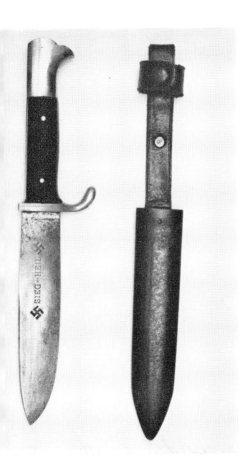
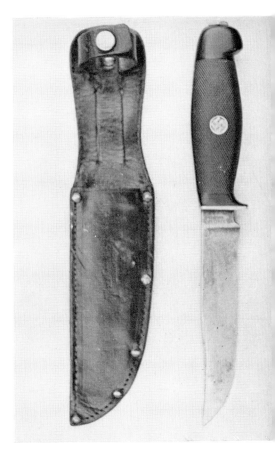

LEFT: Early Nazi sheath knife, identical in size to the HJ Fahrtenmesser, but differing in the plain hilt, and swastika blade motto. Pieces such as this, and other variations, were commonly manufactured during the early 1930s, but after the coming to power of the NSDAP, regulations were enforced determining that only government-sponsored, or approved organisations were permitted to display the swastika on their wares. RIGHT: Sheath knife manufactured by the Bowker company, having brass swastika inset in the black checkered grip; like the previous item, production of this type was phased out after 1933.

FOLLOWING PAGE, TOP:

LEFT: Pre-war paper knives, manufactured in the style of the Naval Dirk, though devoid of the swastika emblem. The example on the left of the photograph is shown complete in its original leatherette case.

RIGHT: Sheath knife, having a finely etched blade commemorating Reich Party Day in Nuremburg, 1935.

Major John R. Angolia collection

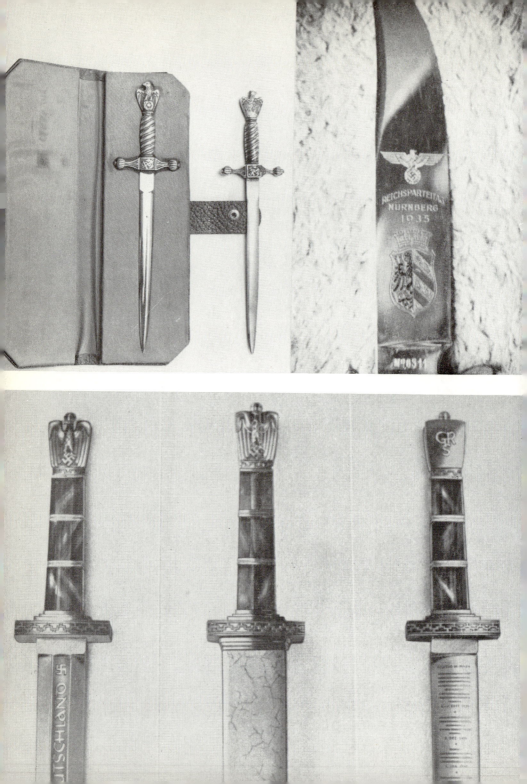

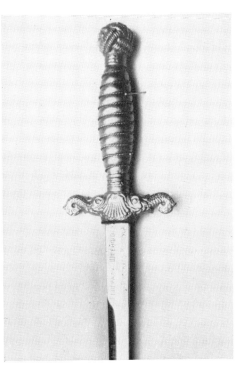

ABOVE AND RIGHT:
This highly unusual dagger may be seen on exhibition in the Army Museum, Brussels. It is basically a First World War period Austro-Hungarian dagger, fitted with German Army suspension straps, and having the unusual blade inscription: 'General Schtenfony, from the Free Russian Army, 1942'. Schtenhfony was a Russian Vlasovite Officer, who worked with troops in collaboration with the Germans.

Photos by Brian L. Davis

OPPOSITE, LOWER:
A selection of prototype sword designs, destined for production, but which never passed beyond the prototype stage. These pieces, representing Army sword patterns, have been reproduced from the publication *Blank Waffen*, published in 1941 by the Solingen Chamber of Commerce. Solingen was the major centre for sword and edged weapon production.

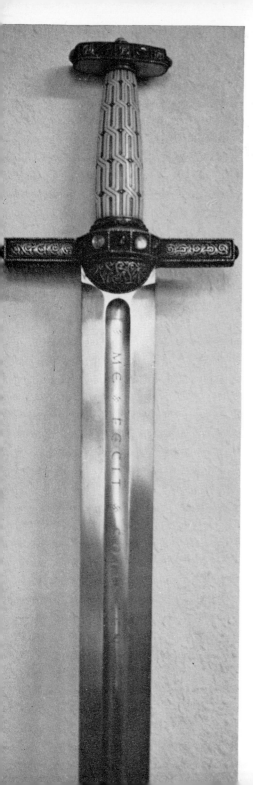

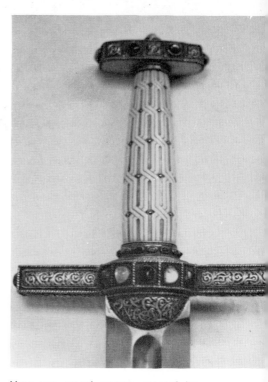

Very rare sword pattern, created by Professor Woenna. This piece is believed to have been one of two such swords produced, and the design is based upon an early German execution sword. The grip is finely engraved ivory, and the hilt is decorated silver, inset with semi-precious stones. The blade is straight and square tipped, and bears in the fuller the etched dedication *Me Fecit Solingen* ('Solingen Created Me'), interspaced with swastikas. The sword was kindly made available to the author by the Director of the Deutsche Klinges Museum, Solingen, which possesses the sole surviving example. It is not on public exhibition, but may be examined on application to the Director of the Museum.

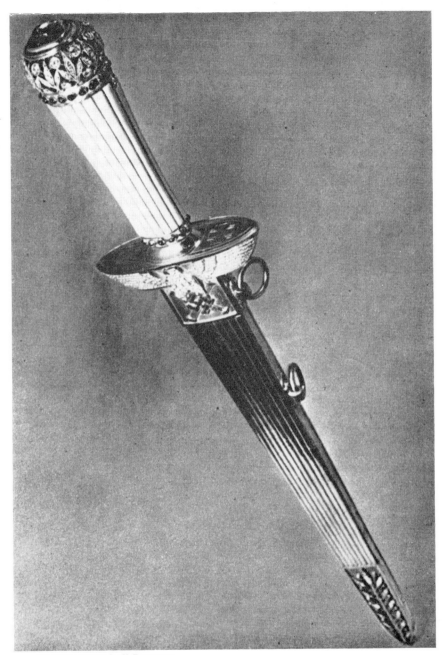

Reichsmarschall Dagger
The dagger manufactured by students of the Berlin Technical Academy, under the direction of Professor Herbert Zeitner, and presented to Göring on the occasion of his being promoted to the rank of Reichsmarschall of the Greater German Reich. The pommel is inset with precious stones, and the Reichsmarschall's emblem forms the crossguard. *Photo T. S. Law*

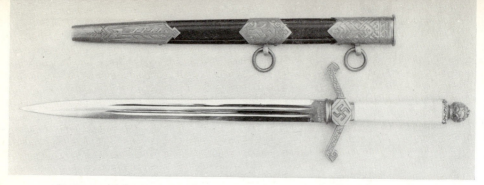

German manufactured dagger produced as the service dress weapon for the Latvian armed forces. The metal fittings are cast brass, showing on the pommel a stylised pine cone, and the swastika on the crossguard. The scabbard fittings are pressed brass, bearing symmetrical ornamentation, with the swastika on the central mount. First produced in 1938, a number of variations to this dagger pattern are known, some having a coat of arms on the reverse of the quillon block, some having the arms enamelled, and yet others having a blank panel. Two manufacturers of the dagger are recorded, the firm of Horster (as illustrated), and Carl Eickhorn. The scabbard is black leather. No further details are known. *Barry Smith collection*

Select Bibliography

The Daggers and Edged Weapons of Hitler's Germany, Major James P. Atwood, Berlin, 1965.

German Daggers and Sidearms of World War II, Dr K-G. Klietmann, Falls Church, Virginia, 1968.

Daggers of the German Third Reich, Andrew Mollo, London, 1967.

Daggers of the Third Reich, Raidl and Leslie, Ohio, 1958.

German Daggers, ZM Research, 1958.

Daggers of the Third Reich, John R. Ormsby, Charlotte, North Carolina, 1971

Feldgrau (continuing series), published by Ordenssammlung, Berlin.

Swords of Hitler's Third Reich, Major John R. Angolia, published by F. J. Stephens, 1969.

Daggers, Bayonets and Fighting Knives of Hitler's Germany, Major John R. Angolia, California, 1972.

A Guide to Nazi Daggers, Swords and Bayonets, F. J. Stephens, Bury, Lancs, 1965.

Eickhorn Kundendienst, sales catalogue of the Eickhorn Company, Solingen, 1938.

Klaas Catalogue, (reprint) 1971, by Mauerer/Hickox, USA.

Paul Seilheimer, sales catalogue of the Seilheimer Company, Solingen, 1938.

German Relics, Stan Bozich, Michigan, 1967.

Der Adler, magazine, published Kansas USA, up to 1969.

Militaria, published by Deeter & Odegaard, Los Angeles, 1969–1971.

Militaria Collector, magazine, published Militaria Publications, London, 1970–1971.

Der Hakenkreuz (Military Collectors News), Pub. Jack Britton, Tulsa, Oklahoma.

Blank Waffen, published by Solingen Chamber of Commerce, 1941.

Leisten und Dienen, published by Carl Eickhorn, Solingen, c. 1940.